I knowed not i'sa free.

African American live slave recordings before emancipation through death.

Illustrated and Edited By Gregory Newson

Why I, Gregory Newson, Am Uniquely Qualified To Speak On the WPA Project

As an author/painter/graphic artist, I, Gregory Newson, am uniquely positioned to discuss on the Works Progress Administration, the program created by the Roosevelt administration in the 1930s to employ out-of-work U.S. citizens during the Great Depression.

In particular, I can share perspectives on the Slave Narratives aspect of the Federal Writers' Project of the WPA to record the experiences of slavery as recalled by former black slaves.

This is in part because, in 2015, I took part in a past-life regression therapy experiment tailored for the Civil War.

Also known as PLR, this form of therapy was developed by psychologists and psychiatrists to rely on hypnosis to resurrect memories from previous lives or reincarnations to treat mental illness. Some policy makers and scientists consider the therapy form controversial because its lack of reliance on formal research.

My session retrieved potent memories and incarnations of living as a slave/ex-slave in the near post-slavery era in the Deep South. My reveries make for compelling testimony about the accuracy of historical lived experiences and the scientific validity of PLR.

The session was directed and supervised by Dr. Joseph Mancini Jr., a certified clinical hypnotherapist. Dr. Mancini has made the practice of PLR the center of his books, "The Present Power of Past Lives: The Experts Speak" and "Ending the Endless Conflict: Healing Narratives from Past-Life Regressions to the Civil War," both published in 2017.

During a typical PLR session, I entered a deep state of relaxation called a trance with suggestions from Dr. Mancini. I was then guided through visualization to something that resembled a door, which, when I opened it, I stepped across a threshold, which led me into a past-life landscape.

After temporarily merging with my past-life self, I communicated and experienced several scenes. As spirit, the past-life self then ascends to the Light to meet guides who discuss the relevance of the life just ended for the life of the present-day individual. After the past-life spirit, which was I, the person named George dissociates from that of the present self. The latter personality returns to present consciousness with aid from the hypnotherapist.

Dr. Mancini and Gregory then debrief the experience. Below is the excerpt of the session from the book "The Present Power of Past Lives."

When Gregory approaches the door, he notices it is four feet tall by three feet wide and made of wood with speckled, oak-white bark. He can see a medium-bright light coming through the slits between the pieces of wood. Intuitively, he knows that he would have to grasp the knob on the right side and push the door to open it.

However, he is very hesitant to touch the knob, which, along with the rest of the door, is crawling with spiders and covered with webs.

Though he thinks about kicking the door open to avoid being bitten, he finally grasps the knob and opens the door very quickly, steps over the threshold and, at my suggestion, looks down at his feet. "I'm barefooted [sic]," he announces as he is now fully George, the past-life self. His medium-to-dark brown feet are clean.

All he has on is an "itchy" garment made out of a burlap bag that, he says, "goes up my whole body" but has no sleeves.

The bag had been cut to make arm holes and one opening for his head. There are no markings or scars on his arms, wrists, and hands though his palms have some open and some scabbing wounds from picking cotton.

Using his hands, under whose nails is black dirt, he examines his long, thin, hairless face with lips blistered from a lack of water. He realizes he is a 12-year-old boy. Only later does he realize he is mulatto.

Outside, standing on dirt and trying to avoid stepping on stones, possibly to avoid their heat from the blazing sun, he senses he is looking around "for danger or something." Though he is alone, he hears in the distance "some noise and activity." He cannot see what is going on because he cannot see past the nearby field of cornstalks which are, he says, "taller than me."

Finding himself next to a slave house with dirt floors, he senses that the "activity" is surrounding the house. As a result, he says, "I don't feel safe ... Something is invading ... the area."

"I'm trying to figure out which way to run," he says. Such an occurrence has not happened before and he feels "trapped." The nearby activity is neither going away nor coming closer. Yet, his fear soon becomes so intense that he says he wants to step back through the doorway and find the stairway that Gregory had descended.

But when he goes back, the stairway is gone, and he finds only darkness. He wants now, he says, to "find a friend or find my mother. Find someone." But, to do so, he realizes he has to go back into the scene and thus does so. Still, he looks to see if he can crawl under the house.

However, there is no crawl space and, thus, he says, "I either have to go left, right, or straight ahead." Suddenly, he hears children about his age who are moving about 50 feet away from him and screaming instructions to each other about finding safety so he decides to follow their voices.

When he reaches them through the cornfield, they motion to him to follow them. "They're without parents, too. No parent, no adults," he says. "I think something very bad has happened to some adults. To their parents ... or mine ... "

The children do not speak more because they must now be quiet and stay in the tall grass or corn. Among the children are a little Negro girl, two White males and one White female. The Whites are about his age though she is the oldest and seems to be in charge.

She is the Master's daughter whom George knows and gets along with "very well." At the White girl's direction, they are keeping quiet and moving away from the Master's house and finally emerge from the cornfield.

However, what they see first are the bodies of three adult slaves. "I'm too afraid to get too close [sic]. But there's blood and a hole in one and blood is coming out," he says. "I keep running with [the White girl] past the bodies."

By the sound of the Union bugle they hear in the distance, they know the soldiers killed the Negroes who were, he says, "trying to protect the property, resisting ... we were just as afraid of the Union Army ... as anything. There's nothing more we were afraid of." After a while, George stops and cries. "[I'm] asking [the other children] about my parents," he says. "Parent—only one. My mother." But there is, sadly, nothing that can be known about his mother's fate. In the next scene, about five hours later during an evening rain, he is inside a main house on another plantation far from the one he had called home. By the candlelight, he can see broken windows and overturned chairs. "Things are broken and ransacked [sic]," he says. "We're looking for something to eat."

The Union soldiers had been here, deliberately destroying parts of the property, but they are now gone. One of the White boys is missing and, George says, "Seems like the older girl don't wanna tell us what happened ... I think it has something to do with my mother. "

He suspects all this because, when George asked the girl earlier about his mother, "She just gave me a sad look ... No words, just a very sad look," one that he had never seen from her before and that made him feel "confused." Yet his hunger distracts him until the White girl finds some cornbread and they all eat. The fear returns to him: "I'm so scared I can't go to sleep ... Sleep is the only way I can escape ...."

In the next scene, five years later, George is nearly 17 and alone in the sunshine outside of a blacksmith shop where he works. After the War ended and before he arrived at the blacksmith shop, he had the grisly job of "digging graves." "I helped dig," he says, "a lot of graves" for "rotten corpses."

"There's plenty of bodies all over the place ... all over—everywhere" in Georgia after General Sherman's march to the sea in late 1864. He adds, "I just roamed around looking for handouts and doing blacksmith's work. Digging graves. Plenty of work for that ... Plenty of work ... The thing I liked about digging graves ... I can go through the pockets ... and find things ...watches. With pictures in 'em... Some of them [watches] was [later] robbed from me ... [Others, I] sold them [to "White folks"] for food ... something. But, seemed like, if I had valuables on me, I wasn't hurt [when I was robbed]. They just wanted my values [sic] ... If I had something of value on me, I would live to see another day."

During this period, he realized that he felt it would have been better to live as a slave at least on the plantation with the White girl. As for the Union Army, which had "liberated" him, he said, "I hated them. I hated them ... [I] just lived day for day, but I hated them ... they brought fear and terrible scenes of ... Everything changed. Too much death. "

His extreme dissatisfaction continued even after finding his current job, where, he says, he is often "cursed upon and told I'm stupid," an occurrence that never happened to him when he was on the plantation. In this job, he does a lot of manual labor and learns, not by being taught, but rather by watching, "how to shape metal and shoe horns and chaw tobacca [sic]."

A year later, he discloses more about his blacksmith job, noting that he worked "whenever I could, as long as anybody could tolerate" his youthfulness. In explaining what he means, he says that the blacksmith, another Negro and a drunk who hung around unsavory people, thought George needed toughening up in order to survive. Thinking that George had been "around too many White folks

prior," his boss was "cruel," sometimes with "harsh pushing," but more often with harsh words that he knew hurt George.

Apparently, the boss also did not like George's connection to the Bible: "He didn't believe in the Bible," says George. "I don't know how to read but I always heard Master and his kids talk about the Bible." The boss seemed to prize ungodly anger as well: "I seemed not to get mad enough for him," says George, "especially when the boss was drunk."

In discussing what had happened with the boss, George [talked about doing jailtime] but not for something he did at his blacksmith job. When he was not in the shop, he would go back to the graves even those he himself had not dug:

"I tried to sell some [of them] to a White couple, a couple of watches, and one recognized a watch or something. So they thought it was better to lock me up and take 'em from me than pay me ... It was easy: just accuse me." His concern now is that he is going to be whipped ... and worse: "Because the War's over, they're hanging Negro men...I seen [sic] one hung up on a tree." Looking back, he realizes that he had tried to escape.

Then: "When he [the jailer] opened the gate, I bust [sic] out. Pushed him on the floor, ran for the door, and I was shot...I can [now] see myself laying [sic] on the floor...Constable or sheriff [shot me]. He wasn't a mean man or nothing. But, I knew that punishment [being hanged] was coming to me. I had to get out of there. I wanted some control of what's going to happen to me. There was no control ... I didn't want to be hung."

As I directed George, now a spirit, to ascend to the Light, something unusual and, at first, confusing happened. "I have another chance ... I do have another chance." (The voice that uttered these words seemed a cross between that of George and that of Gregory.)

"When my ... spirit left my body, it didn't ascend," said George. Apparently, for over 150 years, George's spirit remained earthbound, a ghost. Gregory acknowledged, "Matter of fact, that spirit [of George] I feel just entered me [Gregory] the last ten years, maybe 15 years. I [Gregory] was someone completely different until then ... confused, unfocused, undetermined. I feel like that spirit [of George] this time did escape. I [both George and Gregory] did escape."

He added, "The body that was running for the door, that was shot by the sheriff, that spirit ... I [Gregory] picked it up or it entered me or was always around me ... and I've gotten through that door ... A great light. A great freedom ... A freedom that very few have."

When I asked Gregory if he was okay with George's entering into his life, he said, "...either death had to come to me or a new life." "There's [sic] no two ways about it ... I'm so glad he came." Since George saw slavery mostly "as shelter and protection" and "saw the War and the consequences of freedom worse," as "living hell." George brought hope ... [to Gregory who] was living in great danger. George brought to Gregory "survival skills. And awareness that Gregory don't [sic] have it as bad as he thought he did, compared to his community and what my ancestors went through ... hope is greater now."

George's voice again becomes Gregory's: h, nothing. [I can] be that painter, that creative force that tells a human story.

For more go to the website: http://www.LifeTransformingHypnotherapy.com

3

Summary

A very important change occurs when a person "comes to themselves". For me Gregory Newson artist, writer who has chosen to take the road less traveled only after periods of a reckless lifestyle, I came to myself. But some people never come to themselves at all. But I'm glad I learned the hard way that changing your habits can change your life.

Does the pass live recordings of former American slaves before they died matter to anyone? NOW A DAYS we are known by our acquirements, defects and mannerisms in speech, but these peculiarities meant much more to a certain class of Americans during colonial times. The numerous classes of indentured servants, together with the Negro slaves, could be identified by their speech when they ran away. But in today's society if we encountered someone that spoke like the interviewed WPA Federal Writers' Project formal slaves in this book, we would turn our back's on the conversation and walk away. These are the same people that protest for legislations for more civil rights and political power.

After 10 years of participating in civil war reenactments and historical events; The subject of slavery and civil rights is always around me constantly, which encourages me to be ever so vigilant about others civil rights too, But when I chose to listen to the recordings of former African Americans slaves I too became frustrated and felt no connection; But I realized my intolerance from one glance and quick-read of the transcripts and recordings was a contemporary rush to judgment; "I must make that connection to my ancestors". The re-read was constantly telling me "This is not what black America wants to hear." The forte of my ancestral negro orator is decidedly pathetic; he is most effective in the low tones. In his melancholic cast of speech, he has the habit of sometimes chanting or half-singing his words—what his race very characteristically knows as "moaning"; and it has occasionally the most weird and touching effect. . . . "Speaking in parables," But I continue to read over and over, But the reread open that door back to my "Past Life Regression Experiment" in 2015.

I hope you do go to the Congress of library website; there was no single dialect the slaves spoke. They all struggle to speak English from there passing dialects like; Yaruba, Igbo, and Hausa languages, all of which were from tribes in present day Nigeria, which happened to be where most slaves going to the 13 colonies and the West Indies came from. Over time, these languages tended to merge together (with English), and in one particular case a unique language evolved in South Carolina called Gullah.

The idiomatic expressions of the quarters filtered up to the big house with amazing rapidity. Because the slave found such a close congruence between African proverbs and those in the Bible, he was able to pass on to his master many African ex pressions. Antebellum Southerners frequently noted the Africanization of their children by the slaves.

For example, a group of ministers declared in 1847 that "Our children catch the very dialect of our servants, and lisp all their perversions of the English tongue, long before they learn to speak it correctly." Viewing the close inter action of African slaves with white children, Southern leaders encouraged the Christianization of the bondsmen in an effort to halt the Africanization of the South.

I thank God for the Private efforts in the late 1920s to 1930s to preserve the life histories of former slaves accounted before their deaths. But one might question the wisdom of selecting white Southerners, to direct a project involving the collection of data from African Americans former slaves. Yet whatever racial preconceptions white interviewers may have held do not appear to have had an appreciable effect upon the Slave Narrative Collection. The instructions to interviewers emphasized the necessity of obtaining a faithful account of the ex-slave's version of his or her experience. "It should be remembered that the Federal Writers' Project was not interested in taking sides on any question. The worker were instructed not to censor any materials collected regardless of its nature. The organizers constantly reiterated their insistence that the interviews be recorded verbatim, with no holds barred.

On the other hand, while WPA Federal Writers' Project group was keenly sensitive to the importance of establishing adequate rapport with the former slaves, it does not appear that the WPA Federal Writers' Project seriously considered the possibility that African Americans interviewers might accomplish this more effectively than whites. Earlier evaluations of the Georgia narratives had reported that African Americans interviewers appeared "able to gain better insight" than whites and that the interviews obtained by African Americans were "less tinged with glamour." Nevertheless, no special attempt was made to assign African Americans to this task, as had previously been done in Georgia, Florida, and several other states.

President Ronald Reagan said in 1987
"Perhaps we need some outside universal threat to make us recognize this common bond. I occasionally think how quickly our differences worldwide would vanish if we were facing an alien threat from outside this world."

The regional and racial divisions of the American Civil War still plagues us today. Where are the voices of courageous peacemakers?

Do we really as a nation want to divide ourselves into warring camps again when so many paid the price for our freedom?

What does Thomas Stonewall Jackson and Martin Luther King share in common?
Thomas Stonewall Jackson was the seed spreader for all Southern Black Churchers in the Southland of America. Stonewall Jackson defied Virginia law by teaching African American slaves how to read and write and started the first black Sunday school and supported it with part of his paycheck from the civil war battlefields of America to keep it open

One other exemplified courage better was Dr. Martin Luther King, who said cowardice asks the question: Is it safe? Expediency asks the question: Is it political? Vanity ask the question: Is it popular? But conscience asks the question: is it right? And there comes a time when one must take a position that is neither safe, nor politically correct, nor popular-but one must take it simply because it is right, let's take the profit out of race baiting and reward reconciliation.

A native American elder described his internal Civil War in the following manner; inside of me there are two dogs. One of the dogs is mean and evil and fight others all the time. The other dog is good and seeks to live in peace with all. The mean dog attacks the good dog all the time. When asked which dog wins, the native American elder reflected for a moment, and replied, *The one I feed."*

Do You Swear To Tell The Truth, The Whole Truth and Nothing But The Truth, So Help Me God?

Yes from slave witnesses

Interviews were conducted by Congress of Library employees: Fred Dibble, Rheba Beehler, Hermond Norwood, Ruby T. Lomax, Ruby Terrill - John Avery Lomax, Robert Sonkin, Charles Spurgeon Jones, Lewis Wade, George Lomax, John Wesley, Elizabeth Lyttleton, John Avery, Robert Sonkin, John Henry Faulk, Lomax, Mary Elizabeth Barnicle, Lorenzo Dow Turner, Elmer E. Sparks and Unidentified Female Interviewers

I like to thank people that contributed greatly to my maturing life;

My loving wife Lisa Newson, My mother; Girtie Kendricks, Lou Gaudiosi, Gregory and Rasheeda Green, David Chaltas, Scotty and Tammy Myers, Raymond Day, Reginald Quarles, Tanya Ellis Haessly, Pastor Vaughn McLaughlin, Reverend Farley and his loving wife Faith, John Beatty, HK Edgerton and my brother Craig Featherstone.

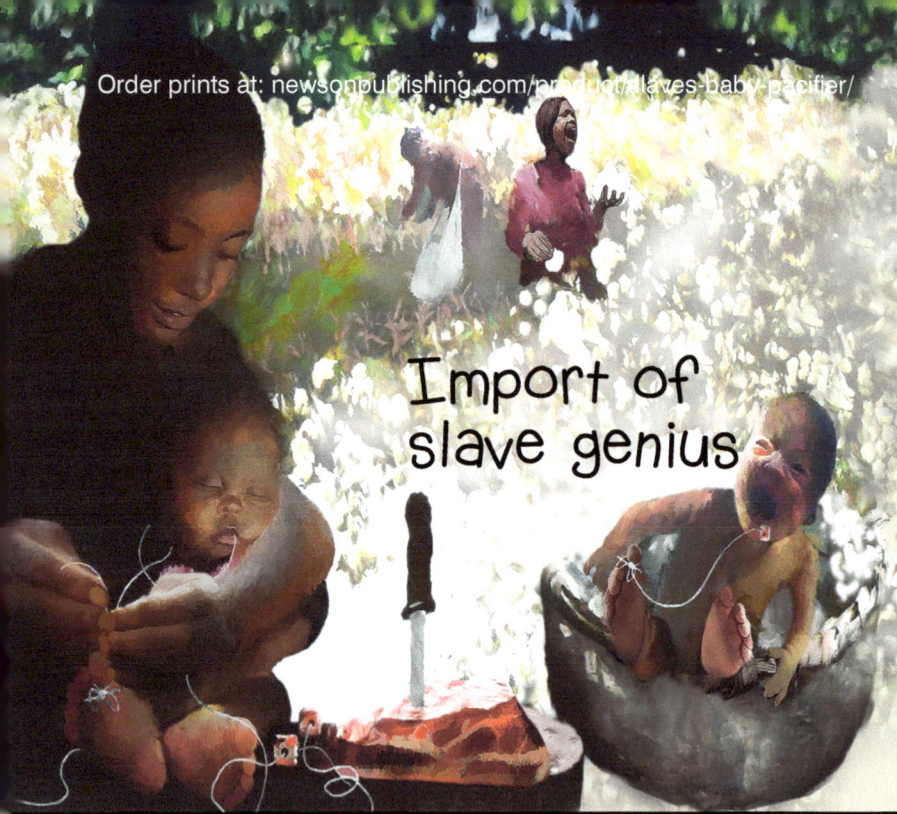

Import of slave genius

The opposite image represents the story a Southern family revealed to this author.

Their great-grandparents, who owned slaves on their plantation, left behind a legacy and knowledge about it to them. As an artist, I was commissioned by Eugene Grady Vickery, a member of The Sons of Confederate Veterans, to interpret and create a painting of a slave's problem-solving and decision-making methods. Such knowledge is not available anywhere else but from white Southerners with slave-owning ancestors.

As an example of how black slaves solved problems and made decisions in their severely confined setting, we take for granted the modern-day baby pacifier we buy from a local supermarket today. A slave used a piece of salt pork to pacify their crying infants when working. In the United States, informal objects were used to pacify babies but the modern pacifier, as we know it, was not invented yet.

During that period, rags with sugar and other pieces of food were used for crying babies throughout Europe and likely the United States and Canada. But chances are, when that new baby was born, the slave still had to work the fields so she went for the next best thing, to invent a pacifier. In those days, a common practice among slaves was to cut a small portion of salt pork, obtain a piece of string, measure it out to the length of the baby's body, use one end to tie the string to the piece of pork and place it into the baby's mouth.

The other end of the string would be tied to the baby's big toe. The slave mother would have the infant sit in a basket of cotton and then return to work in the field. The infant would continue to suck on the piece of salt pork. As the pork shrank, the baby would try to shallow it. This could cause the baby to choke except; that infants under stress tend to stretch themselves out to full length of their bodies.

In turn, the string would be yanked out of the baby's throat and mouth, sparing him or her from choking. This doubled as a pacifier and a lifesaving device so that the slave could go about her work in the plantation, a life would be saved and the slave owner investment advances.

Interview with Mrs. Laura Smalley, Hempstead, Texas, 1941. The WPA interviewed her and here's what she had to say:

Mrs. Laura Smalley: They tend to all the children. Tend to the children. Just like, you know, you bring a whole lot of children, you know, and put them down, you know, at one house. Well, there somebody have to look over them, you know and tend to them that way. Just a house full of them children. And if one act bad, you know, they'd whup them. They'd whup them too, the old woman. And if the old woman didn't tend to the children, they'd whup her too.

Interviewer 1: *Hmm.*

Mrs. Laura Smalley: You know to make her tend to the children, she wasn't doing nothing. Well she wasn't a crippled woman like me, you know. She wasn't an old crippled woman, And they'd whup her. And they had trays, Wooden tray. Dug out, you know, all about that, that long. And all of them you know would get around that tray with spoons, and just eat. I can recollect that because I ate out the tray.

Interviewer 1: *Hmm.*

Mrs. Laura Smalley: With spoons you know, and eat, treat you like mush or soup or something like that. But feed them, you know, before twelve o'clock. And all them children get around there and just eat, eat, eat out that thing. And that old woman, you know, she would tend to them. Her name, Aunt Tishe. Yeah, I know what happen to her. Old woman, name Aunt Tishe.

Interviewer 1: *Just like slopping hogs wasn't it?*

Mrs. Laura Smalley: It just like a tray, you know, just like a tray, you know, you have it's made just like a hog pit, a hog trough, you know.

Interviewer 2: *Hmm, Mrs. Smalley.*

Mrs. Laura Smalley: And, and ah of course you know they'd wash them things and scald them out for the children. I didn't see them scald but that what they told me, they scald them out, you know.

Interviewer 2: *Uhmm.*

Mrs. Laura Smalley: For the children. And them children eat out of that, that thing with wood spoon, if one would, if one reach his spoon over into the other's plate, he going get hit. Hit him, you know. Knock that spoon back, you know, onto his side. And, that's when we was children, you know.

Wasn't able to know other children. I had a brother name, Wright though, he could tend to children. In the, you know, just sit them down in a corner and put this child, you know, little children, put them child in between his leg, and then hug his hand around this child, that's the way he nursed them. Couldn't stand up again him.

I can remember he just shake that child. *Set him in the floor.*

Interviewer 1: *He was too little to pick him up.*

Mrs. Laura Smalley: Yes, sir. And if that child kick much, he'd fall, kick him over too, you know, and the old woman come there and spank them and give him the child back in his arm.

Interviewer 1: [chuckles]

Mrs. Laura Smalley: And they had certain times to come to them childrens. I think about this like a cow out there will go to the calf, you know.

Interviewer 2: *Ahha.*

Mrs. Laura Smalley: And you know, they'd have a certain time, you know, cow come to her calf and at night. Well, they come at ten o'clock. Everyday at ten o'clock to all them babies. Give them what nursing, you know.

Interviewer 2: *Ahha.*

Mrs. Laura Smalley: Them what didn't nurse they didn't come to them at all, the old lady fed them. Them wasn't big, wasn't big enough to eat, you know. She'd ah, the old mother had time, you know to come. When that horn blowed, they'd blow the horn for the mothers, you know. They'd just come just like cows, just a running, you know, coming to the children.

Interviewer 1: *Out of the fields.*

Mrs. Laura Smalley: Out of the fields.

Interviewer 2: *How long did they nurse a baby?*

Mrs. Laura Smalley: Ma'am?

Interviewer 2: *Couple years? How long would they nurse a baby, till it was big enough to walk, I guess?*

Mrs. Laura Smalley: Yes. Something or other like nine months, or something like that, you know.

Interviewer 2: *Ahha.*

Mrs. Laura Smalley: They'd nurse them till they be, get big enough, you know, to eat.

Interviewer 2: *Ahha.*

Mrs. Laura Smalley: Them too get to eat. And they come to, come to every time, come there and ah, nurse that baby, ten o'clock in the day.

Interviewer 2: *During the day?*

Mrs. Laura Smalley: Yes, ma'am. Ten o'clock in the day and three o'clock in the day. They come to that baby and nurse it.

Interviewer 2: *Twice a day.*

Mrs. Laura Smalley: Yes, ma'am, twice a day. Come there and nurse that baby. He couldn't eat you know. But if one didn't eat at dinner time. That old woman had a time in there slopping them children. [laugh] Yes, sir. And I knowed that. And I remember, you see a scar right up in my forehead. Kind of a scar.

Interviewer 1: *Uhmm.*

Interviewer 2: *Yes. Ahha.*

Mrs. Laura Smalley: I had slipped out in the ah, some boys was throwing and knocked this scar in, in on my head when I was little.

Interviewer 2: *Ahha. It's way up here. Right underneath your hairline. Ahha.*

Mrs. Laura Smalley: Yes, ma'am. When I was little. Slipping off out there ah, Old Woman Slopping room. [laugh], I call it. Because you know that's where she fed us.

Interviewer 2: *Ahha.*

Mrs. Laura Smalley: Yes, sir. And that scar, [Pointing with her Finger] because a boy throwed a rock and hit me here. When, when, ah, I was ah young, you know, and hit me. When I was little. Coming out of Old Lady Slop Room.

Interviewer 2: *Hmm.*

Mrs. Laura Smalley: What I'm tell was in a house, you know, where we are feed all the children. I call that a slop room place.

Interviewer 2: *Hmm.*

Mrs. Laura Smalley: Fed all the children.

Interviewer 1: *Now, who did the cooking for the plantation?*

Mrs. Laura Smalley: I don't know what the old woman's name done the, the cooking. A Miss Clemens did tell me not, not long ago, who done the main cooking. But you know they didn't cook in the kitchen like here; [Referring to her present location] they'd had a off, off kitchen. Off from the house.

Interviewer 2: *On the outside, ahha.*

Mrs. Laura Smalley: Yes, ahha. And then pass the vittles, you know, to the kitchen.

Interviewer 2: *Uh huh.*

Mrs. Laura Smalley: Pass it to the kitchen. They didn't have, they wasn't cooking in the, in the kitchen dining room. I was great big girl when I knowed the Mrs. Bethany and them had a kitchen in the dinning room mixed together. I was a big old girl even.

Interviewer 1: [laugh]

Mrs. Laura Smalley: They cooked, you know, on the out side.

Interviewer 2: *Uh huh.*

Mrs. Laura Smalley: Right in the yard out there, and then brought it to the house. They always brought it to their kitchen, when I was a child.

Interviewer 2: *And they had some of the slaves who worked in the house and then some who worked on the yard, isn't that right?*

Mrs. Laura Smalley: No ma'am. They, ah, them work in the yard. Men work in the yard.

But them that worked in the kitchen, they didn't have nothing to do in the yard. And they had one, someone makes up beds you know. And one to cook. And then the girls, had six at time make up bed and then they go to field. And they had regular nurse, you know. Nurse you never did see with the baby. Never no time.

Interviewer 2: *Uhmm.*

Mrs. Laura Smalley: It's like, you know, when you'd hire somebody's nurse, but it be a grown woman nurse. Tend to that baby. And they keep, Now if it was hungry at night or day, and I doubt it was hungry, they carry it there to her. She tend to that baby. That baby slept with the old nurses and all.

Interviewer 1: *Hmm.*

Mrs. Laura Smalley: Yes, has slept with them. Didn't have nothing to do but carry that baby and uh, and ah, sit there until, it nurse. And then after he'd nurse, you know, then, you'd carry it back tend to it. You didn't have to, this, she tend to it, you know, and give it to you.

You'd get, give it to her and nurse it, care how cold it is, and you'd carry that baby back on into that bed. That room where you was.

Interviewer 2: *Hmm.*

Mrs. Laura Smalley: And I know Mrs.

Interviewer 2: *Well, did the mistress nurse the baby, or did she have a?*

Interviewer 1: *Yeah.*

Mrs. Laura Smalley: She, she nursed from the breast.

Interviewer 2: *Ahha.*

Mrs. Laura Smalley: But see, she'd nursed this baby that, that it would still be hungry. Well, this here, nurse would bring it to her, and let her nurse it.

And then when she nurse she'd hand it right back, night or day, you know. Had tend to that baby night and day and hand it back her. And that baby with any kind of sick that nurse had to sit up there at night and tend to it.

Interviewer 2: *Uh huh.*

Mrs. Laura Smalley: Yes, ma'am. Well, more than.

Interviewer 2: *You never did, eh?*

Mrs. Laura Smalley: Ma'am?

Interviewer 2: *You never worked in care of it like that?*

Mrs. Laura Smalley: No.

Interviewer 2: *What the nurse had to do?*

Mrs. Laura Smalley: No. Well, you see that's done now right here.

Interviewer 2: *Ahha*

Interviewer 1: That's right.

Mrs. Laura Smalley: Folks now done now right here. Oh, my niece at, grand daughter here, she take care of baby, and they can mother her a little, take care and do slave time too. [laugh]

Interviewer 1: *Hmm.*

Interviewer 2: *Yeah, I know it.*

Mrs. Laura Smalley: She never do hardly,... let her take it.

Interviewer 2: *I know a lot of women dealing with someone elses.*

Mrs. Laura Smalley: Yes, ma'am. Don't send for her, you know.

Interviewer 1: *Well, do you remember, remember any of the slaves being sold? Do you remember any slave sellers, you know, men that would just buy and sell slaves?*

Mrs. Laura Smalley: No, sir. I never did see it. Why I never, us children never did know that, you know. We heard talk of it, but then I reckon that was after, after slavery I reckon. We heard talk of it. I used to hear them talk about, you know, you putting them on stumps, you know. Or something high, you know and bidding them off like you did cattle.

Interviewer 1: *Hmm.*

Mrs. Laura Smalley: Bid them off like you did cattle.

Interviewer 1: *Well, none of your folks were ever sold then?*

Mrs. Laura Smalley: No, sir. None of them never was sold.

Interviewer 2: *You were born right there and never did leave. You were?*

Mrs. Laura Smalley: Born right there and stayed there until I was about nine, ten years old, maybe more. Stayed right there. We didn't know where to go.

Interviewer 2: *Uhmm.*

Mrs. Laura Smalley: Mama and them didn't know where to go, you see after freedom broke. Just turned, just like you turn something out, you know. Didn't know where to go. That's just where they stayed.

Interviewer 2: *Uh huh. That's right.*

Mrs. Laura Smalley: Hmm. Didn't know where to go. Turned us out just like, you know, you turn out cattle. [laugh] I say. Didn't know where to go.

Interviewer 1: *You remember when the Civil War was being fought?*

Mrs. Laura Smalley: Well, I, I can't remember much about it, but I remember this much: When uh, Mr. Bethany was gone a long time. Look like a long, long, time. And I remember all the next morning, when he, he got up. Well, ah, he and we all got up and all of us went to the big house to see old massa . And I thought old massa was dead, but he wasn't. He had been off to the war, and ah, come back. But then I didn't know, you know about the war. I just know he was gone a long time. All the niggas gathered around to see the old massa again. You know, and old massa didn't tell you we are free.

Interviewer 1: *He didn't tell you that?*

Mrs. Laura Smalley: Uh-uh. No he didn't tell. They worked there, I think now they say they worked them, six months after that. Six months. And turn them loose on the nineteenth of June. That's why, you know, we celebrate that day. Colored folks celebrates that day.

Mrs. Adeline, our mistress, you know. And just catched her by her wrist this way, you know. Both of them pushed down in a rocking chair. And when she, Mrs. Dapheny, come home she was crying. And Mrs. Dapheny asked her what was the matter, you know. She told Mrs. Adeline that Martha Albert hurt her, hurt her wrist. And ah, and she, asked her then, then told her. [Pointing a finger] "What you doing in this house here hurting old mistress?"

Martha say, she wasn't hurting old mistress. She used to old mistress, when "I help her she started down." But, but the thing that old woman, poor old woman carried on. They took Martha Albert to the peach orchard and, and whupped her. And, you know, just tied her hands this way, you know, around the peach orchard tree.

I remember that just as well what it, look like to me I can around the tree and whupped her.

Well, she couldn't do nothing, but just kick. Just kick her feet. But they had her clothes off pull to her waist, you know. Yes, didn't have her plum naked. But they had her clothes down to her waist. And every now and then they'd whup her. You know, and then, snuff the pipe out on her, you know. Snuff the pipe out on her. You know, with thee embers in the pipe. I don't believe we ever seen the pipe smoking.

Interviewer 1: *Blow them out on her?*

Mrs. Laura Smalley: Hmm. Hmm.

Interviewer 1: *Good god.*

Mrs. Laura Smalley: Hep

Interviewer 1: *Did she scream?*

Mrs. Laura Smalley: Yeah! I think she was. I think she did. But you see there was we was daring to go out there, where it was, you know. Because ah, our old massa would whup us and then, Uncle Saul would whup us too.

You see, that is the overseer, Uncle Saul. Her papa was a overseer but he had to whup her. He whupped her too. He really sure did whup her. Well he ah whup ped her so that at night they had to grease her back. Grease her back. I didn't know what kind of grease we had, but they sure greased her back, at night you know, that way. We just grease her back. And ah, so after him, after so long on them, such whupping being so long, that when they quit. They quit and give her her dinner, and course she beening whupped so bad then, you know, she didn't want to eat, you know. If for they whupped you half a day, you ain't want to eat, you know too.

Interviewer 1: [laugh] *That's right.*

Mrs. Laura Smalley: Because a little child, you can whip a little child here now, it get mad, you know, and don't want to eat nothing. He won't eat. So one time Uncle Saul, him, he, was going whup my momma's brother, oldest brother named, Cal Heck. And he was going whup de boy, and she was going fight them. [laugh]

Interviewer 1: *Is that right?*

Mrs. Laura Smalley: Yes, sir. She was going fight them. You see one portion of the people belonged to Mr. Bethany, and one portion, you know, belongs to, belongs to his wife. Wife, you know, just like, you know, you have a lot of niggas, you know, and they give you a portion of them, and your wife aportion of them.

Her people give you people, people for them and your people give you some. Well that makes two parts. You got a part and your wife got a part, you know.

Interviewer 1: *Uhmm. Uhmm.*

Mrs. Laura Smalley: Of colored folks that way. And, so Mrs. Adeline wouldn't let my Uncle Saul whup him. That was her side, you know. That wasn't her nigga, she wouldn't let Uncle Saul whupher, that way. But ithey call her a sassy nigga. That's what they call wouldn't let Uncle Saul whup her too.

Interviewer 1: *Hmm*

Mrs. Laura Smalley: All day and if Uncle Saul stayed late, you know, when they got to the water spot where Uncle Saul was, those field were, they was pitching out, as fast as children could get to them. You know. And she whup them if they let them.

Interviewer 1: *Hmm.*

9

Mrs. Laura Smalley: Yeah, she whup them if they let them. Now, and so, Uncle Bethany, you know, he wasn't my daddy, he wasn't, wasn't ah.

Interviewer 2: *He's your daddy?*

Mrs. Laura Smalley: Uhmm. He wasn't, now don't let me? He, he wasn't born, he wasn't, he wasn't married to Bethany' niggas, you see. He was a Pane.

Interviewer 1: *Pane?*

Mrs. Laura Smalley: My old stepdaddy, yeah. He was a Pane. Uhmm. He was a Pane. And ah, he'd do everything, you know, he, he would, they couldn't whup him. Tha' man couldn't whup him. And his head, [Pointing to her hair] his head was red it was red.

Interviewer 1: *Well, where'd he come from?*

Mrs. Laura Smalley: Well, I think he come from at Louisiana. Somewhere. Anyhow, he come from somewhere. Couldn't exactly care where he come from. Because my momma come from Mississippi.

Interviewer 1: *Yes, he was rail thin.*

Interviewer 2:: *Rail thin.*

Mrs. Laura Smalley: Yes, sir. Yes, Yes ma'am.

Interviewer 1: *Yes.*

Mrs. Laura Smalley: He's a giant big old man, you know, what I mean?

They wouldn't let them whup him, you see. And the massa wouldn't let them hurt him, because he let you know, the ah, overseer, you know, they whup you. The massa make him whip you, what overseer do when you see them.

And they wouldn't let overseers whup him at all, oh no. And their old massa told him, run in the, or something like that, don't hurt him. You know, don't. Don't whup him. He wouldn't whup him. Well, I tell you something, no he wouldn't whup him.

Interviewer 1: [laugh]

Mrs. Laura Smalley: No, sir. He wouldn't whup him.

Interviewer 1: *Well how would they punish him then?*

Mrs. Laura Smalley: Give him a ear of corn. [laugh] Give him ear of corn. Just like, you know, you give them a ear of corn and ah that'll get for my dinner, or or breakfast.

You come home to dinner you give him ear of corn. Night come and they give him ear of corn, and ah, tha's the way they fed him, you know. Punishing him, you know. Wouldn't give him nothing to eat. Until he look like he was moving along too slow you know.

10

Interviewer 2: [laugh]

Mrs. Laura Smalley: Too good for that, you know, just giving him corn. And he's eating it and drink water go on just the same. That's so they wouldn't give him *none*. Give him *none*.

Interviewer 2: Hmm.

Mrs. Laura Smalley: They wouldn't give him *nothing*, you know. But they let them drink water, you know. And ah, he lived just the same. And you, and he, he lived with momma twenty, thirty-two years, that before he died. Before he died. And, and he never did had a scar on him, my father, the old boss put on him.

Interviewer 1: What approximately they paid for your step daddy? How come ah, ah?

Mrs. Laura Smalley: No Paid, you know. Just, he wasn't a Pane. They said Prade, but he was what you call them? But you see, I don't know what they paid for him; they paid for him, you know.

Interviewer 1: *And, I guess he was worth so much they didn't want to hurt him.*

Mrs. Laura Smalley: Didn't want to hurt him. And ah, he ah, you see, he had belonged to two, two sets of folks. Two sets, of people, you know. And he had, he, he would belongs to a Pane, then he belongs to a, some people, you know, in Brenwood. They all stayed with the, you see he wouldn't, wouldn't do right and they'd sell him. They'd sell him, you know. Just like, you know, out here old nigga, you know, I wouldn't act right sell me to to somebody else.

And wouldn't act right what they would be for not being a good hand, you sell him to somebody else. That's the way they would do that nigga.

Interviewer 1: *I see.*

Mrs. Laura Smalley: They traded down.

Interviewer 1: *Well, what about getting married? How did they go about marrying the slaves?*

Mrs. Laura Smalley: Well, they told me they jumped over a broom backward. [laughter from all]

Interviewer 1: *Well, did they have church? Did the slaves have a church?*

Mrs. Laura Smalley: Oh, oh, I, I never remember no church. Momma said, we're all in church, I didn't remember that part of it. All in church. And would have be a tub, tub of water, sitting just like this thing is, [Pointing at tub] you know, and that would catch your voice. And they would, they would have church around there tell them all to get around the tub. Get around that tub.

Interviewer 1: *Old massa didn't want them in the church.*

Mrs. Laura Smalley: We don't have no church. No. We didn't have no church because. And um, old massa come along in one of them, one was ah, was there, having church around the tub and we was down praying.

And say he's down and he prayed and just a prayed and old massa come in and we just a prayed and he come in and he say to me all, "Get up from there." We didn't get up, we just praised. And old massa couldn't.

We kept pray in and asking the "Lord have mercy on my massa . Lord have mercy on old massa . Lord have mercy on old massa ." Say, "I thought sure i getting my butt whupped."

Interviewer 1: *Hmm.*

Mrs. Laura Smalley: That's how we get mercy for old massa. I'm dealing with massa . Folk didn't even care for him wouldn't get up, you know. Just flinch, you know, flinch. Got a person, you know, when person hit you, you know, you flinch. You just pray for old massa .

Old massa step back and fell dead in line and kick you. and kick you. When ever you stop praying, you know, he, he said, "Go on head and pray."

Interviewer 1: *Hmm.*

Mrs. Laura Smalley: Said, "Go on head and pray." Because we wouldn't stop. And that was for the Lord, you know, that's because of that.

Interviewer 1: *Yeah, the Lord works a lot of things.*

Mrs. Laura Smalley: Yeah, sir. Because the Lord will suffer, we stay down there get that whupping where we prayed. You know, just keep up praying. You know, I think I jumped up. I didn't know. No way for me I jumped up. Because a whupping was—

END OF SIDE B

At another end of the spectrum, virtually all masters and mistresses saw the value of a high reproductive rate and encouraged or coerced their slaves to start large families.

Fertile females, sometimes called "breed women" by the former slaves, often received special treatment—light work, good food and a welcome period for rest and rehabilitation.

However, barren women ran the risk of being sold, for as one Alabama slave put it, "Iffen she ain't er good multiplier dey gwine ter git shut er her rail real soon."
For a much smaller number of planters, interference took on more direct forms.

Some masters or mistresses supervised the pairings among their slaves and encouraged or even required a "fine and stout" man to marry a similarly-built woman.

Centuries later, these type of forced marriages frequently broke up with the end of slavery. On other plantations, especially small holdings with an excess of women, the master used a "stockman," "travelin' nigger," or a "breedin' nigger."

"Durin' slavery, there were stockmen," one slave explained in a narrative. "They was weighed and tested. A man would rent the stockman and put him in a room with some young women he wanted to raise children from."

Detailing the financial arrangements involved, another slave said that the owners of the male slave "charged a fee of one out of every four offspring for his services."

The "breedin' nigger" could be from the same plantation and simply have access to more than one woman or the master might reward "de big man" or an especially valuable hand on the plantation with more than one wife in hopes of raising some "fine, portly children."

Forced interracial sex was much more frequent, according to both white and black sources. A woman from South Carolina of a high social status described plantations as "brothels" and said, "We live surrounded by prostitutes."

She blamed these arrangements on white male planters and plantation owners and many former slaves concurred with her assessment.

For example, one slave owner said, "at dat time it wus a hard job to find a master dat didn't have women 'mong his slaves. Dat wus a ginerel thing 'mong de slave owners." Some perverse individuals, possibly male members of the planter's family, made slave men yield their place in bed and gave friends access to the women on the plantation. Although no one will ever be able to quantify the amount of interracial sex that occurred on such plantations in the Old South, it is apparent that it happened often enough to produce substantial numbers of mulatto children.

While unrelated, many former slaves intermarried with Indians more commonly than is often recognized but the former slaves reported far more instances of race-mixing with whites.

Of course, some white-black liaisons involved true love or pursuit of status or advantage by the slave.

As one slave woman revealed to researchers, "Some did it because they wanted to." But coercion underlay most instances.

This same informant added, "They had a horror of going to Mississippi and they would do anything to keep from it." In the face of all the seemingly insurmountable odds of survival and quality of life, questions naturally arise about the viability of the slave family.

Forced sex, interracial relationships, and the total authority of the master all threatened the black family but the greatest danger was the separation of established families, due primarily to sales.

Roughly one-fifth of the former slaves interviewed for narratives about slavery—as collected by the Library of Congress under the Depression-era WPA project—had experienced at least one partial breakup of their families during slavery, according to historical federal research.

For more of this interview go to: https://www.loc.gov

LIBRARY OF CONGRESS

| Everything ⌄ | Laura Smalley |

Sword down they just make them, sword down, and they just lay down their sword, and squash them down.

Interview with Wallace Quarterman, Fort Frederica, St. Simons Island, Georgia, June 1935 and here's what he had to say.

Description: Wallace Quarterman, a son of slaves about the end of the war:

Wallace Quarterman: *[in the beginning of this interview he quotes religious scripture]* The Lord gave the whole earth my grace with thee.

Interviewer 1: *Uh huh.*

Wallace Quarterman: For them that do and trust my word he shall be saved. But he that won't believest shall go to hell!

Interviewer 2: *Uh huh.*

Wallace Quarterman: I make him great commission. Know that he who preach my gospel truth by all the work that him can do, that's all the wonder I will do.

Interviewer 2: *Uh huh.*

Wallace Quarterman: You must teach all nation my command, I am with you until the world shall end. Well I think that's enough, I had enough!

Interviewer 2: *Uh humm. Okay.*

Wallace Quarterman: Okay *[short pause before Wallace Quarterman sings]*

Wallace Quarterman: I Surrender Oh, let me come on i-in. I surrender and open the door. Let me come in open up. Yeah, let me come i-inn. Oh, let me come i-i-i-innn. I surrender, yes open the door, and let me come in. I said baby don't you cry, mothers and father are born to die. I surrender. Oh, let me come i-inn. I surrender and open the door and let me come in.

Wallace Quarterman: *[heavy cough, singing stops]* I can't sing much. Down South getting mighty poor. Say they, used to drink coffee but now they drinking rye. They said, let music Union Band make the rebel understand. To leave our land for the sake of Uncle Sam. Way down South getting mighty poor. Shot at the wildcat and see the Rebel run. I ain't going anywhere them see me again. I've been to war already.

Interviewer 2: *humm. Okay*

Wallace Quarterman: Yeah, yeah. And that, the people then throw away their hoes. They throwed away they hoe, and, and they call we all up, you know and, and give we all freedom because we are just as much as free as them.

Now you understand. But the Yankees saying we must go back to the South they'll help we. Well, they didn't. Of course, there was so much doubt, and it seems to me I, they would have done more, but it so much doubt in the way. They couldn't because the colored people sure been poor, and some white people sure went poor too.

You understand and they rather help them than, uh, help we. I satisfied so far, for the Lord has done for me, I come through, through all the, been up and downs through thee.

Interviewer 2: *Well tell me about how they went to Hawkinsville and drove the sword down in the ground?*

Wallace Quarterman: *They told them, said now you.*

Interviewer 2: *After they said you can go free, then what did you do? Did you run on off the plantation that day? Did you leave the plantation that day after they told you to go free?*

Wallace Quarterman: That day Massa promised so, to give we forty dollars a month in pay. The lot said the boys said they ain't want it. They rather go free you know.

Interviewer 2: *Humm.*

Wallace Quarterman: Well, of course not, why I have them pay me, you understand? I get along with them you know. Massa brought out the big pot, you know.

Interviewer 2: *Yeah.*

Wallace Quarterman: And ah, after they, after this place closed down, sword down they just make them, sword down, and they just lay down their sword, and squash them down. You go in Hawkinsville and you see all the swords down now.

Interviewer 2: *Yeah (?)*

Wallace Quarterman: In the ground. And after the sword was down the tension, in the South tension. And after the South tension then they play. Yeah. Play they. [*he thumbs a washtub base Instrument and sings*] Kingdom Coming One foot one way. One foot the other way. One foot all around. Jumping. Standing. Couldn't cut a figure. And he couldn't go halfway around. Old Massa run away. And set them darkies free.

For you must be think thy kingdom a coming in the hour of jubilee. So we had a big breaking up right there, you know, after it. That's right.

Interviewer 1: *What about afterwards? You know when the colored people had the be jailer and everything? Tell us about that.*

Wallace Quarterman: Yes, wehen everything been in we hands. But they couldn't control the colored people. They do so much mischief until we have to go on back to the white people who had education. You know when a man ain't got no education he ain't got nothing. All we tried to show them they wouldn't they just kill one another and going on.

So we had to nominate democrats over they heads. They didn't like it many got killed by nominate the democrat, but we couldn't help it, had to stop them, so much killing. You understand?

Interviewer 1: *Humm.*

Wallace Quarterman: So we nominate the democrat, and we had a big time from that till now.

Interviewer 1: *Humm.*

Wallace Quarterman: The times ain't bad now because we beat them.

Interviewer 1: *Humm.*

Wallace Quarterman: Because a man thinks nothing killing,.. a man as if taking a drink of water.

Interviewer 1: *Humm.*

Wallace Quarterman: But since we nominate the democrat we have more assurance. You understand.

Interviewer 1: Yes.

Wallace Quarterman: The law come in protecting them, you know they wouldn't yell at the colored people.

Interviewer 2: *Yeah.*

Wallace Quarterman: At all ma'am, at all.

Interviewer 2: *Mhmm.*

Interviewer 2: *What was his name?*

Wallace Quarterman: Colonel Fedwary.

Interviewer 2: *Fedwary?*

Wallace Quarterman: Yes. And he was a colonel.

Interviewer 2: *Mhmm.*

Wallace Quarterman: I wouldn't take anything, why me and he was just like one, you know.

Interviewer 2: *Yes.*

Wallace Quarterman: Yes, ma'am.

Interviewer 2: *Well, where was his plantation?*

Wallace Quarterman: His plantation on, on Savannah River. You know, Skidaway Island?

Interviewer 2: *Humm.*

Wallace Quarterman: And he had another one in Chattum County, you know. Savannah.

Interviewer 2: *Yeah.*

Wallace Quarterman: Skidaway Island.

Interviewer 2: *Humm.*

Wallace Quarterman: And umh, yes, sir, I wouldn't take nothing from him.

Interviewer 1: *Well, did the white folks like it when you all were in power?*

Wallace Quarterman: Oh, they liked me. They would like me all the way, because I protect them, you know.

Interviewer 1: *Yes.*

Wallace Quarterman: I protect them I told them, I told them when the Yankee come myself and they didn't feel sorry for them you know. You see I just would understand how they think, you know.

Interviewer 1: *Yes.*

Wallace Quarterman: Tell me things you know.

Interviewer 1: *Ahha.*

Wallace Quarterman: I see a man going to do a wrong thing I should stop it though. I stop him. Why?

Interviewer 2: *Well, did the white people, did your Massa and all them, like to see the Negroes be the judge and the jailer and everything?*

Wallace Quarterman: Whooo! You see according to law you know, they don't mind you be that, I mean, if you know what you doing.

Interviewer 2: *Humm.*

Wallace Quarterman: Don't you see?

Interviewer 2: *Yes.*

Wallace Quarterman: Yeah. We, we, you see, they, they don't know what they doing..

Interviewer 2: *Yeah.*

Emancipation: Promise & Poverty

In the antebellum Deep South, life after slavery opened up a whole new world for African Americans. Gone were the whippings, incidents of sexual assaults, the selling and forcible relocation of family members and other gross injustices. African Americans celebrated their newfound freedom both privately and publicly.

But life in the years after slavery also proved difficult. Although slavery was over, the brutalities of white racial prejudice persisted. After slavery, state legislatures across the South instituted laws known as the Black Codes.

The Black Codes were meant by racist state lawmakers to regiment newly-freed African Americans in all aspects of their lives and relegate them to second-class citizenship status. To empower their ranks, African Americans created such political organizations as the Union League.

During Reconstruction, the Union League was the main vehicle for mobilizing the newly-enfranchised voters for the Republican Party. The League originated during the Civil War as a white patriotic organization supporting the Union war effort.

It was generally secret and oath-bound. With the end of the war, Republican leaders decided that the clandestine nature of the organization made it appropriate to launch political operations against white Southerners. Under a series of laws enacted to intimidate blacks, tens of thousands of African Americans were arbitrarily arrested, hit with outrageous fines, and charged for the costs of their own arrests.

With no means to pay these ostensible "debts," prisoners were sold as forced laborers to coal mines, lumber camps, brickyards, railroads, quarries, and farm plantations.

Thousands of other African Americans were simply seized by Southern landowners and compelled into years of involuntary servitude. Government officials leased falsely imprisoned blacks to small-town entrepreneurs, provincial farmers, and dozens of corporations—including U.S. Steel—looking for cheap and abundant labor.

Armies of "free" black men labored without compensation, were repeatedly bought and sold, and were forced through beatings and physical torture to do the bidding of white masters for decades after the official abolition of American slavery.

The neoslavery system exploited legal loopholes and federal policies that discouraged prosecution of whites for continuing to hold black workers against their wills. As it poured millions of dollars into Southern government treasuries, the new slavery also became an instrument in domestic terrorism against African Americans seeking full participation in the U.S. political system and the economy.

Based on a vast record of original documents and personal narratives, a book titled Slavery by Another Name unearths the lost stories of slaves and their descendants who journeyed into freedom after the Emancipation Proclamation and then back into the shadow of involuntary servitude.

It also reveals the stories of those who fought unsuccessfully against the re-emergence of human labor trafficking, the companies that profited most from neoslavery, and the system's final demise in the 1940s.

But he ran off from him, too, and come to Major Flannigan's in Rusk County.

ANDERSON AND MIKERVA EDWARDS,
a Negro Baptist preacher and his wife, were slaves on adjoining plantations in Rusk County, Texas and Anderson was born March 12, 1844, a slave of Major Matt Gaud, and Minerva was born February 2, 1850 a slave of Major Flannigan.

As a boy Anderson would get a pass to visit his father, who belonged to Major Flannigan, and there he met Minerva. They worked for their masters until three years after the war, then moved to Harrison County, married, and reared sixteen children. Anderson and Minerva live in a snail but comfortable farm house two miles north of Marshall. Minerva's memory is poor, and she added little to Anderson's story.

Description: The WPA interviewed ANDERSON AND MIKERVA EDWARDS in Rusk County, Texas, and here's what they had to say:

ANDERSON: My father was Sandy Flannigan and he had run off from his first master in Maryland, on the east 'shore, and come to Texas, and here a slave buyer picked him up and put chains on him. If they could find his Maryland master, he'd had to go back to them and if they couldn't the chances was good.

Wash Edwards in Panola County bought the chains and him, but he ran off from him, too, and come to Major Flannigan's in Rusk County.

Fin'ly Major Flannigan had to pay a good lot to get clear title to him. "My mammy was named Minerva and her master was Major Grand, and I was born there on his plantation in 1866.

You can ask that tax man at Marshall '"bout my age, 'cause he's fix my 'exemption papers since I'm sixty. I had seven brothers and two sisters. There was Frank, Joe, Sandy gad Gene, Preston said William and Sarah and Delilah, and they all lived to be old folks and the youngers just died last year.

Folks was more healthy when I growed up and I'm 93 now and ain't dead, fact is, I feels right part mos' the time. My missy named Mary and she and Massa

Matt lived in a hewed log house, which still standin out there near Henderson. Our quarters was cross the road and set all in a row. Massa own three families of slaves and lots of horses and sheep and cows in my father herded for him till he was freed. The government run a big tan yard there on Major Gaud's place and one of my uncles was shoemaker.

Just bout time of war, I was piddlin' 'round the tannery and a government man say to me, Boy, I'll give you $1,000 for a drink of water, and he did, but it was confederate money that's no got, so it done me no good.

Mammy was a weaver and made all the clothes and massa give us plenty to eat; fact, he treated us kind-a like his own boys. Course he whipped us when we had to have it, but not like I see darkies whipped on others in other places.

The other niggers called us Major Gaud's free niggers and we could hear 'em moanin' and cryin' round 'bout, when they was puttin' it on 'em. I worked in the field from one year end to other and when we come in at dusk we had to eat and be in bed by nine. Massa give us mos' anything he had to eat, 'cept biscuits.

That ash cake wasn't such bad eatin and it was cooked by putting cornmeal batter in shucks and bakin' in the ashes.

We didn't work in the field Sunday but they have so much stock to tend it kept us busy.

Minerva got 'religious and all so took us to church when she could. When we prayed by ourselves we daren't let the white folks know it and we turned a wash pot down to the ground to catch the voice. We prayed a lot to be free and the Lord done heared us.

We didn't have no song books and the Lord done give us our songs and when we sing them at night it's just whispering so nobody hear us. One went like this;

'My knee bones am aching, My body's rackin' with pain, I believe I'm a chile of God, And this ain't my home, Cause Heaven's my aim.

Massa Gaud give big corn shuckin's and cotton pickin's and the women cook up big dinners and massa give us some whiskey, and lots of times we shucked all night. On Saturday nights we'd sing and dance and we made our own instruments, which was gourd fiddles and quill flutes.

Gen'rally Christmas was like any other day, but I got Santa Claus twice in slavery, 'cause massa give me a sack of molasses candy once and some biscuits once and that mean a whole lot to me then.

The Vinsons and Frys what lived next to massa sold slaves and I seen 'em sold and chained together and druv off in herds by a white man on a horse. They'd sell babies way from the mammy and the Lord never did 'tend sick as that.

I believe in that haunt business yet, I see one when I was a boy, right after momny die. I woke up and see it come in the door, and it had a body and legs and tail and a face like a man and it walked to the fireplace and lifted the lid off a skillet of 'taters what set there and came then to my bed and raised up the cover and crawled in and I hollers so loud it wakes everybody.

I tell em I see a ghost and they say I crazy, but I guess I knows a haunt when I sees one.

Minerva can tell you 'bout that haunted house we lived in near Marshall jus' after we's married.

Minerva Edwards: Deed, I can tell you her story. The next year after Anderson and me marries we moves to a place what had belonged to white folks and the man was real mean and choked his wife to death and he left the country and we moved in.

We heared peculivar noises by night and the niggers round there done told us it was haunted but I didn't believe 'em, but I do now. One night we seed the woman who was died come all 'round with a light in the hand and the neighbors said that candle light the house all over and it look like it on fire.

She come every night and we left our crop and moved away from there and ain't gone back yit to gather that crop, before we moved in that place been empty since the woman die, 'cause nobody live there. One night Charlie Williams, what lives in Marshall, and runs a store out by the T. & P Hospital got drunk and goes out there to sleep and while he sleepin' that same woman come in-and choked him to death. Ain't nobody ever live in that house since we is there.

Anderson Edwards: I 'member when war starts and Massa's boy George, he say, saddles up ole Bob, his pony, and he left. He stays six months and when he ride up back Massa say, 'How's the war, George say, 'It's Hell. Me and Bob has been runnin' from Yankees ever since us lef'.' fore war. Massa didn't never say much 'bout slavery but when he heered us free he cusses end say, 'Gawd never did 'tend to free niggers,' and he cussed till he died.

But he didn't tell us we's free till a whole year after we was, but one day a bunch of Yankee soldiers come ridin' up and massa and missy hid out. The soldiers walked into the kitchen and mammy was churnin' and one of them kicks the churn over and say, 'Git out, you's jus as free as I is. Then they ramsacked the place and breaks out all the window lights and when they leaves it look like a storm done hit that house.

Massa come back from hidin and that when he starts on a cussim spree what lasts as long as he lives.

Bout four year after that war pappy took me to Harrison County and I've lived here ever since and Minerva's papy moves from the Flannigan place to a jimin farm bout that time mid several years later we was married.

It was at her house and she had a blue serge suit and I wore a cutaway Prince Albert suit and they was bout 200 folks at our weddin. The next day they give us an affair and a big dinner.

We raises sixteen chillen to be growed and six of the boys is still livin and workin' in Marshall, I been preaching the Gospel and formin' since slavery time.

I joined de church mos' 83 year ago when I was Major Gaud's slave and they baptizes me in the spring branch clost to where I finds the Lord.

When I starts preachin' I couldn't read or write and had to preach what massa told me and he say tell them niggers if they obeys the massa they goes to Heaven but I knowed there's something better for them, but dare not tell them cept on the sly. That I done lots. I tells em they kepps prayin' the Lord will set 'em free.

But since them days I's done studied some and I preached all over Harrison County and I started the Edward's Chapel over there in Marshall and pastored it till a few year ago. It's named for me.

"I don't preach much now, cause I can't hold out to walk far and I got no other way to go. We has a $14.00 pension and lives on. that and what we can raise on the farm.

According to many slave narratives and recordings, a slave who made the fateful decision to escape from his or her master's property with the North Star as a guide had to overcome nearly impossible odds.

His greatest challenge was the psychological pain and sorrow he would endure of leaving behind home, family and friends he or she knew and loved. In the case of a male slave, his mothers and wives would argue vigorously against his departure.

As many of his peers would have said in the era, "Blessed be the ties that bind." The decision was a dangerous or a potentially life-changing one and a slave had to think long and hard before pondering embracing his freedom.

In particular, he had to weigh and consider the danger that lay ahead of him. He would have to think about his chances of actual escape and the tragic risk of failure, his fear and ignorance of the unknown, particularly the world around him and geography.

The slave also would have to ponder his impoverished state, his inability to trust any white man and his master's past warnings of the consequences of such a plot. Many slaves discussed making their way to Canada but admitted that one would have to summon up all of the superhuman courage and determination he or she had to choose this route.

A slave once confessed that it pained him most to leave all he knew still in slavery and to abandon a faithful wife, children, other family members and friends, especially with a gut-wrenching, emotional parting.

He also had to consider the blame, collective punishment and other consequences his family would all face at the hands of the master or overseer for his escape. In his narrative and recording, he talked about having to suppress his feelings and to muster all the emotional wherewithal he had to do so.

The night before or of his escape, a slave would describe his set of circumstances at having to make such a giant leap in the dark. He would also have to take into account the utter lack of protection that federal and state law afforded a slave in the Southern states. On huge plantations, by law and in actuality, all power and authority was vested in a slave's overseers.

Overseers were expected to enable the plantation owners or planters they served to turn over as much profit as possible. They achieved this by intimidating the slaves to boost productivity.
More likely than not, inducements to maximize profit included corporal punishment against the slaves.

Overseers came under severe pressure and nearly all of the time resorted to whipping slaves in an effort to increase profits. Sometimes, they would mutilate or brand slaves towards this end. In one such typical anecdote, an overseer from a tobacco plantation had a wooden leg and would sneak up on the slaves to hear what they spoke about in his absence.

The loudness of his peg leg would give him away when he was walking towards and was enroute to approaching his slaves. The slaves knew him well and they were familiar with his conniving, underhanded, cruel and sadistic manner. As a result, he was roundly and thoroughly disliked by them all.

His misdeeds included brutally whipping them. As an example, this particular overseer would force a slave remove his shirt, tie his hands behind his back and heaped 100 lashes on it. The offense? The slave was missing three pounds of product from his quota of work, which amounted to six cents.

For more of this interview go to: https://www.loc.gov

LIBRARY OF CONGRESS

Everything ⌄ | Anderson Edwards

Massa say from top de tree, "I'sa come to take you home with me".

Interview of Willis Easter, 35, born near Nacogdoches, Texas, He does not know the name of his first master, Frank Sparks brought Willis to Bosqueville, Texas, when he was two years old.

Willis believes firmly in "conjure men" and ghosts, and wears several charms for protection against the former.

Willis Easter: I's birthed below Nacogdoches, and dey tells me it am on March 19th, in 1852.

My mammy had some kind of paper what say date. But I don't know my Massa cause when I'sa two he done give me to and he bring me to Bosque-Ville.

Dat sizeable place My mammy come bout a month after, cause Massa Frank, he say dem days. I'sa too much trouble without my mammy.

Mammy de best cook in de county and a master hand at spinning and weaving.

18

She made her own dye.

Walnut and elm makes red dye and walnut brown color, and Shumaker makes black color. When you want yellow color, git cedar moss out de brake.

All de lint was picked by hand on our place. It's a slow job to git dat lint out de cotton and I's gone to sleep many a night, settin by de fire, pickin lint. In bad weather us sot by de fire and pick lint and patch harness and shoes, or whittle out something, dishes and bowls and troughs and traps and spoons.

All us chillen weared lowel white duckin, homemade, jes one garment. It was de long shirt. You couldn't tell gals from boys on de yard.

I's twelve when us am freed and for awhile us lived on Massa Bob Wortham's place, on Chalk Bluff, on Horseshoe Bend after de freedom war dat old Brazos River done change its course up above de bend, and move to de west.

I marries Nancy Clark in 1879, but no chilluns. Dere plenty deer and bears and wild turkeys and antelopes here den, and wish I could stick a tooth in one now. I's seed fifty antelope at a water in hole.

I can remember he just shake that child. Set him in the floor.

Interviewer 1: *He was too little to pick him up.*

Mrs. Laura Smalley: Yes, sir. And if that child kick much, he'd fall, kick him over too, you know, and the old woman come there and spank them and give him the child back in his arm.

Interviewer 1: [chuckles]

Mrs. Laura Smalley: And they had certain times to come to them childrens. I think about this like a cow out there will go to the calf, you know.

Interviewer 2: *Ahha.*

Mrs. Laura Smalley: And you know, they'd have a certain time, you know, cow come to her calf and at night. Well, they come at ten o'clock. Everyday at ten o'clock to all them babies. Give them what nursing, you know.

Interviewer 2: *Ahha.*

Mrs. Laura Smalley: Them what didn't nurse they didn't come to them at all, the old lady fed them. Them wasn't big, wasn't big enough to eat, you know. She'd ah, the old mother had time, you know to come. When that horn blowed, they'd blow the horn for the mothers, you know. They'd just come just like cows, just a running, you know, coming to the children.

Interviewer 1: *Out of the fields.*

Mrs. Laura Smalley: Out of the fields.

Interviewer 2: *How long did they nurse a baby?*

Mrs. Laura Smalley: Ma'am?

Interviewer 2: *Couple years? How long would they nurse a baby, till it was big enough to walk, I guess?*

Mrs. Laura Smalley: Yes. Something or other like nine months, or something like that, you know.

Interviewer 2: *Ahha.*

Mrs. Laura Smalley: They'd nurse them till they be, get big enough, you know, to eat.

Interviewer 2: *Ahha.*

Mrs. Laura Smalley: Them too get to eat. And they come to, come to every time, come there and ah, nurse that baby, ten o'clock in the day.

Interviewer 2: *During the day?*

Mrs. Laura Smalley: Yes, ma'am. Ten o'clock in the day and three o'clock in the day. They come to that baby and nurse it.

Interviewer 2: *Twice a day.*

Mrs. Laura Smalley: Yes, ma'am, twice a day. Come there and nurse that baby. He couldn't eat you know. But if one didn't eat at dinner time. That old woman had a time in there slopping them children. [laugh] Yes, sir. And I knowed that. And I remember, you see a scar right up in my forehead. Kind of a scar.

Interviewer 1: *Uhmm.*

Interviewer 2: *Yes. Ahha.*

Mrs. Laura Smalley: I had slipped out in the ah, some boys was throwing and knocked this scar in, in on my head when I was little.

Interviewer 2: *Ahha. It's way up here. Right underneath your hairline. Ahha.*

Mrs. Laura Smalley: Yes, ma'am. When I was little. Slipping off out there ah, Old Woman Slopping room. [laugh], I call it. Because you know that's where she fed us.

Interviewer 2: *Ahha.*

Mrs. Laura Smalley: Yes, sir. And that scar, [Pointing with her Finger] because a boy throwed a rock and hit me here. When, when, ah, I was ah young, you know, and hit me. When I was little. Coming out of Old Lady Slop Room.

Interviewer 2: *Hmm.*

Mrs. Laura Smalley: What I'm tell was in a house, you know, where we are feed all the children. I call that a slop room place.

Interviewer 2: *Hmm.*

Mrs. Laura Smalley: Fed all the children.

Interviewer 1: *Now, who did the cooking for the plantation?*

Mrs. Laura Smalley: I don't know what the old woman's name done the, the cooking. A Miss Clemens did tell me not, not long ago, who done the main cooking. But you know they didn't cook in the kitchen like here; [Referring to her present location] they'd had a off, off kitchen. Off from the house.

Interviewer 2: *On the outside, ahha.*

Mrs. Laura Smalley: Yes, ahha. And then pass the vittles, you know, to the kitchen.

Interviewer 2: *Uh huh.*

Mrs. Laura Smalley: Pass it to the kitchen. They didn't have, they wasn't cooking in the, in the kitchen dining room. I was great big girl when I knowed the Mrs. Bethany and them had a kitchen in the dinning room mixed together. I was a big old girl even.

Interviewer 1: [laugh]

Mrs. Laura Smalley: They cooked, you know, on the out side.

Interviewer 2: *Uh huh.*

Mrs. Laura Smalley: Right in the yard out there, and then brought it to the house. They always brought it to their kitchen, when I was a child.

Interviewer 2: *And they had some of the slaves who worked in the house and then some who worked on the yard, isn't that right?*

Mrs. Laura Smalley: No ma'am. They, ah, them work in the yard. Men work in the yard.

But them that worked in the kitchen, they didn't have nothing to do in the yard. And they had one, someone makes up beds you know. And one to cook. And then the girls, had six at time make up bed and then they go to field. And they had regular nurse, you know. Nurse you never did see with the baby. Never no time.

Interviewer 2: *Uhmm.*

Mrs. Laura Smalley: It's like, you know, when you'd hire somebody's nurse, but it be a grown woman nurse. Tend to that baby. And they keep, Now if it was hungry at night or day, and I doubt it was hungry, they carry it there to her. She tend to that baby. That baby slept with the old nurses and all.

Interviewer 1: *Hmm.*

Mrs. Laura Smalley: Yes, has slept with them. Didn't have nothing to do but carry that baby and uh, and ah, sit there until, it nurse. And then after he'd nurse, you know, then, you'd carry it back tend to it. You didn't have to, this, she tend to it, you know, and give it to you.

You'd get, give it to her and nurse it, care how cold it is, and you'd carry that baby back on into that bed. That room where you was.

Interviewer 2: *Hmm.*

Mrs. Laura Smalley: And I know Mrs.

Interviewer 2: *Well, did the mistress nurse the baby, or did she have a?*

Interviewer 1: *Yeah.*

Mrs. Laura Smalley: She, she nursed from the breast.

Interviewer 2: *Ahha.*

Mrs. Laura Smalley: But see, she'd nursed this baby that, that it would still be hungry. Well, this here, nurse would bring it to her, and let her nurse it.

And then when she nurse she'd hand it right back, night or day, you know. Had tend to that baby night and day and hand it back her. And that baby with any kind of sick that nurse had to sit up there at night and tend to it.

Interviewer 2: *Uh huh.*

Mrs. Laura Smalley: Yes, ma'am. Well, more than.

Interviewer 2: *You never did, eh?*

Mrs. Laura Smalley: Ma'am?

Interviewer 2: *You never worked in care of it like that?*

Mrs. Laura Smalley: No.

Interviewer 2: *What the nurse had to do?*

Mrs. Laura Smalley: No. Well, you see that's done now right here.

Interviewer 2: *Ahha*

Interviewer 1: That's right.

Mrs. Laura Smalley: Folks now done now right here. Oh, my niece at, grand daughter here, she take care of baby, and they can mother her a little, take care and do slave time too. [laugh]

Interviewer 1: *Hmm.*

Interviewer 2: *Yeah, I know it.*

Mrs. Laura Smalley: She never do hardly,... let her take it.

Interviewer 2: *I know a lot of women dealing with someone elses.*

Mrs. Laura Smalley: Yes, ma'am. Don't send for her, you know.

Interviewer 1: *Well, do you remember, remember any of the slaves being sold? Do you remember any slave sellers, you know, men that would just buy and sell slaves?*

Mrs. Laura Smalley: No, sir. I never did see it. Why I never, us children never did know that, you know. We heard talk of it, but then I reckon that was after, after slavery I reckon. We heard talk of it. I used to hear them talk about, you know, you putting them on stumps, you know. Or something high, you know and bidding them off like you did cattle.

Interviewer 1: *Hmm.*

Mrs. Laura Smalley: Bid them off like you did cattle.

Interviewer 1: *Well, none of your folks were ever sold then?*

Mrs. Laura Smalley: No, sir. None of them never was sold.

Interviewer 2: *You were born right there and never did leave. You were?*

Mrs. Laura Smalley: Born right there and stayed there until I was about nine, ten years old, maybe more. Stayed right there. We didn't know where to go.

Interviewer 2: *Uhmm.*

Mrs. Laura Smalley: Mama and them didn't know where to go, you see after

Dere plenty Indians, too. De Rangers had de time keepin dem back, Dey come in bright of de moon and steals and kills de stock. Dere a ferry cross de Brazos and Capt. Ross run it. He sho fit dem Indians.

Dera days everybody went horseback and de roads was jes trails and bridges was poles cross de creeks. One day us went to a weddin. Dey sot de dinner table out in de yard under a big tree and de table was a big slab of a tree on legs, Dey had pewter plates and spoons and chiny bowls and wooden dishes. Some de knives and forks was make out of bone. Dey had beef and pork and turkey and come antelope, I knows bout ghosts'. First, I tells you a funny story. A old man named Josh, he putty old and notionate. Every evenin he squat down under a oak tree. Massa Smith, he slip up and hear Josh prayin, 'Oh, God, please take pore old Josh home with you, Next day, Massa Smith' wrap he-self in a sheet and git in de oak tree.

Old Josh come 'long and pray, Oh, God, please come take pore old Josh home with you. Massa say from top de tree, Poor Josh, I'sa come to take you home with me. Old Josh, he riz up and seed de white sheet in de tree, and he yell, Oh Lord, not right now, I hasn't git forgive for all my sins. Old Josh, he jes' shakin and he dusts out dere faster den a wink. Dat broke up he prayin under dat tree.

"I never studied conjuring, but I knows dat scorpions and things dey conjures work with is a powerful medicine. Dey uses hair and fingernails and tacks and dry insects and worms and bat wings and insect.

Mammy allus tie a leather string round de babies' necks when dey teethin. to make dem have easy time. She used a dry frog or piece of nutmeg too. Mammy always tell me to keep from be inl conjure, I sing:Keep 'way from me, hoodoo and witch, Lend my path from de poorhouse gate; I pines for golden harps and sich, Lord, I just set down and wait.   Old Satan am a liar and conjurer, too

If you don't watch out, he'll cunjure you.- If you don't watch out, he'll cunjure you.-men sho' bad. Dey make you have pneuraony and boils and "bad luck, I carries me a jack all de time. It's my charm wrop in red flannel. Don't know what em in it bossman, he fix it for me.

I sure can find water from de well. I got a li'l tree limb what am like a V. I driv de nail in de end of each branch and in de crotch. I takes hold of each branch and iffen I walks over water in de bound, dat limb gwine turn over in my hand till it points to de ground. Iffen money am buried, you can find it de same way.

"Iffen you fills a shoe with salt and burns it, dat call luck to you. I wears a dine on a string round de neck and one round de ankle. Dat to keep any conjure man from sottin' de trick on me. Dat dime be bright iffen my friends am true.

For more of this interview go to: https://www.loc.gov

| Everytthing | ⌄ | Willis Easter | 🔍 |

Throughout the African diaspora both here and abroad, there is cultural and philosophical overlap in black religious and spiritual practices and beliefs.

For example, in the days before British and European colonialism in what we now know as the Congo Republic in central Africa, African tribes saw the world as a many-sided structure with two mountains connected to their bases and cut by a horizontal line, symbolized by water.

The tribesmen thought that humans would die and their spirits would "travel to the other side," a land resembling the world of the living. The only difference is that, they believed, their ancestors, ghosts and spirits lived there all of the time but were able to influence lives in the previous world.

In the United States, for centuries after the first slaves were shipped and arrived from Africa, all religious practices and beliefs were combined into one voodoo faith.

With all of the different varieties of African gods and goddesses from throughout the motherland, the slaves focused on the snake god of the Whydah, Fom and Ewe when they struggled to continue the worship rites of their predecessors from the old continent.

Representing the rainbow and the umbilical cord that connects a mother to her newborn infant, slaves believed the snake stood for all changes in life in general.

Back in Africa, the snake represented the god of fertility, good and ill fortune. It was believed a person could only call up the god's protective spirit by worshipping him.

In 19th century Louisiana, many slaves and some whites worshipped the snake god Dam balla.

The voodoo priests and priestesses believed they had the power to make masters kind to slaves, hurt enemies, guarantee love and make the sick whole again.

The priests and priestesses had many worshippers and often supervised their reportedly wild orgies in ceremonies on the shores of New Orleans.

Without question, slaves, researchers and scholars have been able to trace and point to the African origins of African-American Protestant Christian religion, including its aspects of the use of rhythm, the "shout," "call and response," spiritual dance and trance.

However, what is not as clearly stated is the connection between African religion and African-American supernatural traditions such as "conjure."

Researchers and scholars looked to material objects in black culture in both Africa and the United States for evidence of this relationship. Some say the making of physical charms in the United States are a prime example of the connection between both worlds.

For instance, "voodoo" dolls and figures, seen in religious rite shops in New Orleans and Miami, have been compared to similar physical relics and icons in the Congo Republic and in Benin and Togo, West Africa.

Still, African spirituality and religion doesn't just live on in black American supernatural beliefs and practices.

It also presents in African-American ideas about the divine and about cause, effect, how spiritual forces react to humans and how worshippers honor their dead.

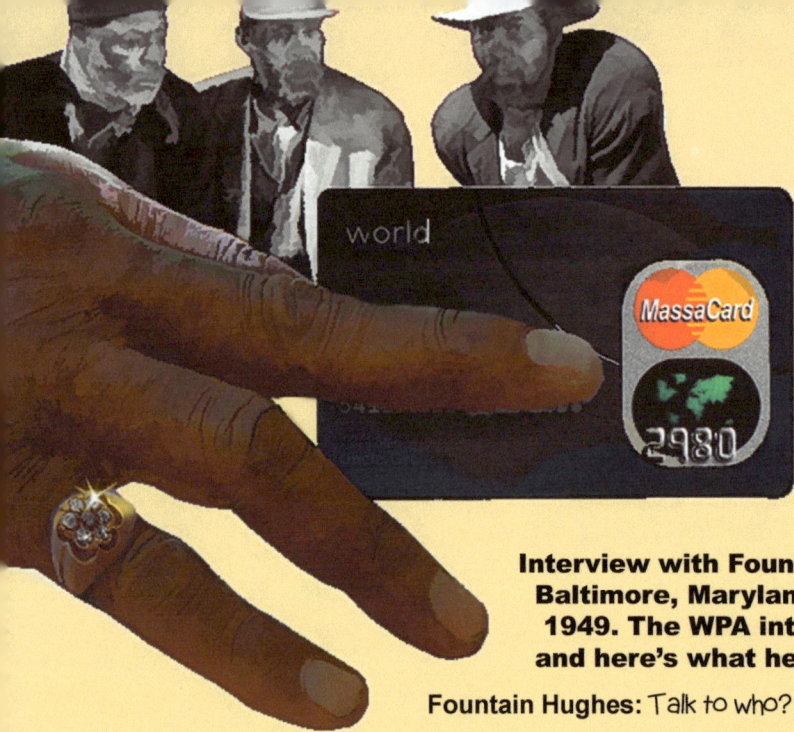

Interview with Fountain Hughes, Baltimore, Maryland, June 11, 1949. The WPA interviewed him and here's what he had to say:

Fountain Hughes: Talk to who?

Interviewer: *Well, just tell me what your name is.*

Fountain Hughes: My name is Fountain Hughes. I was born in Charlottesville, Virginia. My grandfather belong to Thomas Jefferson. My grandfather was a hundred and fifteen years old when he died. And now I am one hundred and, and one year old. That's enough. He used to work, but what he made I don't know. I never ask he.

Interviewer: *You just go ahead and talk away there. You don't mind, do you, Uncle Fountain?*

Fountain Hughes: No. And when, now, your husband and you both are young. You all try to live like young people ought to live. Don't want everything somebody else has got. Whatever you get, if its yours be satisfied. And don't spend your money till you get it. So many people get in debt. Well, that was so cheap when I bought it.

You spend your money before you get it, because you're going in debt for what you want. When you want something, wait until you get the money and pay for it cash. That's the way I've done. If I've wanted anything, I'd wait until I got the money and I paid for it cash. I never bought nothing on time in my life. Now plenty people if they want a suit of clothes, they go to work and they'll buy them on time. Well they say they was cheap. If you got the money you can buy them cheaper. They want something for, for waiting on for, uh, till you get ready to pay them. And if you got the money you can go where you choose and buy it when you go, when you want it. You see? Don't buy it because somebody else go down and run a debt and run a bill or, I'm going to run it too. Don't do that. I never done it. Now,

Debt is fast-becoming a type of modern slavery in the United States. If our federal economic research is to be believed, more people are proving more willing to spend money they don't have on products and services they may not need. Aside from the pervasiveness of debt, racism can take on a covert form unlike in the time of slavery and Jim Crow.

The combination of the two—debt and racism—is lethal. In the 1930s, the federal government under President Roosevelt crafted and enacted the New Deal, a national policy meant to address the economic crisis brought on by the Stock Market Crash of 1929 and the ensuing Great Depression.

Still, the policy led to a segregated and unequal credit market for African American families. Under the New Deal's assortment of program entitlements, banks and other lending institutions retained staff who would charge predatory high interests, installment balances and fees in the low-income black communities. By contrast, lenders would offer low-interest, safe, affordable credit cards and other financial services in predominately white suburbs.

At the time, Congress held hearings and legislative was created with programs that led to new executive orders to fight the crisis.

Their socioeconomic effects on African American communities continue on to this day. After the Civil War, former slaves looked for jobs and planters needed cheap labor. The lack of cash or standalone credit prompted planters and former plantation owners to invent the system of sharecropping. Sharecropping enables a planter and tenants on his farming property to enter into an agreement to use his land for a share of the crop.

The practice allowed tenants to work to generate as abundant a harvest as possible and the planter could tie them to the land as long as possible so they would not pursue other forms of work or means of survival. African-American families rented the land from their white owners and grew the most profitable crops such as cotton, tobacco and rice. In most instances, the owners or local businessmen would have the families rent their equipment and provide seed, fertilizer, food and other materials on credit before harvest time.

During that time, the tenants, the planter or businessmen would settle accounts on debts and how much was owed to whom. High interest rates, swings between harvest gains and losses and dishonest, unethical planters and businessmen would hold whole tenant families hostage with heavy debt, forcing them into this status from year to year. All the laws worked in the favor of the planters and businessmen and made it impossible for sharecroppers to sell their crops to others or to move off the land. Sharecropping trapped black families into an early 20thcentury form of enslavement.

I'm a hundred years old and I don't owe nobody five cents, and I ain't got no money either. And I'm happy, just as happy as somebody that's oh, got million. Nothing worries me. I'm not, my head ain't even white. I, nothing in the world worries me. I can sit here in this house at night, nobody can come and say, "Mr. Hughes, you owe me a quarter, you owe me a dollar, you owe me five cents." No you can't. I don't owe you nothing.

Why? I never made no bills in my life. And I'm living too. And I'm a hundred years old. And if you take my advice today, you'll never make a bill. Because what you want, get your money, pay them cash, and then the rest of the money is yours. But if you run a bill they, well, so much and so much and you don't have to pay. Nothing down it's, it's all when you come to pay. It's all, you don't have to pay no more. But they, they'll, they'll charge you more. They getting something or other or else they wouldn't trust you. But I can't just say what they getting. But they getting something or other else they wouldn't want your credit. Now I tell you that anybody that trusts you for two dollars or you have a account with them by the month or by the week, store count or any account. They're getting something out of it. Else they don't want to accommodate you that much to trust you. Now, if I want, course I ain't got no clothes, but if I want some clothes, I, I ain't got no money, I'm going to wait till I get the money to buy them. Indeed I am. I'm not a going to say because I can get them on trust, I go down and get them.

I got to pay a dollar more anyhow. But either they charge you more or they say taxes are so much. But if I've got the money to pay cash, I'll pay the taxes and all down in cash, you know. It's all done with. So many of colored people is head over heels in debt. Trust me trust. I'll get it on time. They want a set of furniture, go down and pay down so much and the rest on time. You done paid that, you done paid for them then. When you pay down so much and they charge you fifty dollar, hundred dollars for a set and you pay down twenty-five dollars cash, you done paid them. That's all it was worth, twenty-five dollars, and you pay, now you, I'm seventy-five dollars in debt now.

Because I, I have to pay a hundred dollars for that set, and it's only worth about twenty-five dollar. But you buying it on time.

But people ain't got sense enough to know it. But when you get old like I am, you commence to think, well, I have done wrong. I should have kept my money until I wanted this thing, and when I want it, I take my money and go pay cash for it. Or else I will do without it.

That's supposing you want a new dress. You say, well I'll, I'll buy it, but, uh, I don't need it. But I can get it on time. Well let's go down the store today and get something on time. Well you go down and get a dress on time. Something else in there, I want that. They'll sell that to you on time. You won't have to pay nothing down. But there's a payday coming. And when that payday comes, they want you come pay them. If you don't, they can't get no more. Well, if you never do that, if you don't start it, you will never end it. I never did buy nothing on time. I must tell you on this, I'm sitting right here now today, and if I's the last word I've got to tell you, I never even much as tried to buy a, a shirt on time. And plenty people go to work, go down to the store and buy uh, three and four dollars for a shirt. Two, three uh, seven, eight dollars for a pair of pants. Course they get them on time. I don't, no, no, no. I say, I got, I buy something for five dollars. Because I got the five dollars, I'll pay for it. I'm done with that.

Interviewer: *You talk about how old you are Uncle Fountain. Do you, tell how far back do you remember?*

Fountain Hughes: I remember, Well I'll tell you, uh. Things come to me in spells, you know. I remember things, uh, more when I'm laying down than I do when I'm standing or when I'm walking around. Now in my boy days, why, uh, boys lived quite different from the way they live now. But boys wasn't as mean as they are now either. Boys lived to, they had a good time. The masters di, didn't treat them bad. And they was always satisfied. They never wore no shoes until they was twelve or thirteen years old. And now people put on shoes on babies you know, when they're two year, when they month old. I be, I don't know how old they are. Put shoes on babies. Just as soon as you see them out in the street they got shoes on. I told a woman the other day, I said, "I never had no shoes till I was thirteen years old." She say, "Well but you bruise your feet all up, and stump your toes." I say, "Yes, many time I've stump my toes, and blood run out them. That didn't make them buy me no shoes." And I been, oh, oh you wore a dress like a woman till I was, I be-believe ten, twelve, thirteen years old.

Interviewer: *So you wore a dress.*

Fountain Hughes: Yes. I didn't wear no pants, and of course didn't make boys' pants. Boys wore dresses. Now only womens wearing the dresses and the boys is going with the, with the womens wearing the pants now and the boys wearing the dresses. *Still* [laughs].

Interviewer: *Who did you work for Uncle Fountain when... ?*

Fountain Hughes: Who'd I work for?

Interviewer: *Yeah.*

Fountain Hughes: When I, you mean when I was slave?

Interviewer: *Yeah, when you were a slave. Who did you work for?*

Fountain Hughes: Well, I belonged to, uh, B., when I was a slave. My mother belonged to B. But my, uh, but, uh, we, uh, was all slave children. And after, soon after when we found out that we was free, why then we was, uh, bound out to different people. And an all such people as that. And we would run away, and wouldn't stay with them. Why then we'd just go and stay anywheres we could. Lay out a night in underwear. We had no home, you know. We was just turned out like a lot of cattle. You know how they turn cattle out in a pasture? Well after freedom, you know, colored people didn't have nothing. Colored people didn't have no beds when they was slaves. We always slept on the floor, pallet here, and a pallet there. Just like, uh, lot of, uh, wild people, we didn't, we didn't know nothing. Didn't allow you to look at no book. And then there was some free born colored people, why they had a little education, but there was very few of them, where we was. And they all had uh, what you call, I might call it now, uh, jail centers, was just the same as we was in jail.

Now I couldn't go from here across the street, or I couldn't go through nobody's house without I have a note, or something from my massa . And if I had that pass, that was what we call a pass, if I had that pass, I could go wherever he sent me. And I'd have to be back, you know, when uh. Whoever he sent me to, they,

they'd give me another pass and I'd bring that back so as to show how long I'd been gone. We couldn't go out and stay a hour or two hours or something like. They send you. Now, say for instance I'd go out here to S.'s place. I'd have to walk. And I would have to be back maybe in a hour. Maybe they'd give me hour. I don't know just how long they'd give me. But they'd give me a note so there wouldn't nobody interfere with me, and tell who I belong to. And when I come back, why I carry it to my massa and give that to him, that'd be all right. But I couldn't just walk away like the people does now, you know. It was what they call, we were slaves. We belonged to people. They'd sell us like they sell horses and cows and hogs and all like that. Have a auction bench, and they'd put you on, up on the bench and bid on you just same as you bidding on cattle you know.

Interviewer: *Was that in Charlotte that you were a slave?*

Fountain Hughes: Hmmm?

Interviewer: *Was that in Charlotte or Charlottesville?*

Fountain Hughes: That was in Charlottesville.

Interviewer: *Charlottesville, Virginia.*

Fountain Hughes: *Selling women, selling men. All that. Then if they had any bad ones, they'd sell them to the nigga traders, what they called the nigga traders. And they'd ship them down south, and sell them down south. But, uh, otherwise if you was a good, good person they wouldn't sell you.*

But if you was bad and mean and they didn't want to beat you and knock you around, they'd sell you what to the, what was call the nigga trader. They'd have a regular, have a sale every month, you know, at the courthouse. And then they'd sell you, and get two hundred dollar, hundred dollar, five hundred dollar.

Interviewer: *Were you ever sold from one person to another?*

Fountain Hughes: Mmmm?

Interviewer: *Were you ever sold?*

Fountain Hughes: No, I never was sold.

Interviewer: *Always stayed with the same person.*

Fountain Hughes: All, all. I was too young to sell.

Interviewer: *Oh I see.*

Fountain Hughes: See I wasn't old enough during the war to sell, during the Army. And uh, my father got killed in the Army, you know. So it left us small children just to live on whatever people choose to, uh, give us. I was, I was bound out for a dollar a month. And my mother used to collect the money.

Children wasn't, couldn't spend money when I come along. In, in, and fact when I come along, young men, young men couldn't spend no money until they was twenty-one years old. And then you was twenty-one, why then you could spend your money.

But if you wasn't twenty-one, you couldn't spend no money. I couldn't take, I couldn't spend ten cents if somebody give it to me. Because they'd say, "Well, he might have stole it." We all come along, you might say, we had to give an account of what you done. You couldn't just do things and walk off and say I didn't do it. You'd have to, uh, give an account of it. Now, uh, after we got freed and they turned us out like cattle, we could, we didn't have nowhere to go. And we didn't have nobody to boss us, and, uh, we didn't know nothing. There wasn't, wasn't no schools.

And when they started a little school, why, the people that were slaves, there couldn't many of them go to school, except they had a father and a mother. And my father was dead, and my mother was living, but she had three, four other little children, and she had to put them all to work for to help take care of the others. So we had, uh, we had what you call, worse than dogs has got it now. Dogs has got it now better than we had it when we come along. I know, I remember one night, I was out after I, I was free, and I didn't have nowhere to go. I didn't have nowhere to sleep. I didn't know what to do. My brother and I was together. So we knew a man that had a, a livery stable. And we crept in that yard, and got into one of the hacks of the automobile, and slept in that hack all night long. So next morning, we could get out and go where we belonged. But we was afraid to go at night because we didn't know where to go, and didn't know what time to go.

But we had got away from there, and we afraid to go back, so we crept in, slept in that thing all night until the next morning, and we got back where we belong before the people got up. Soon as day commenced, come, break, we got out and commenced to go where we belonged. But we never done that but the one time. After that we always, if there, if there was a way, we'd try to get back before night come. But then that was on a Sunday too, that we done that. Now, uh, when we were slaves, we couldn't do that, see. And after we got free we didn't know nothing to do. And my mother, she, then she hunted places, and bound us out for a dollar a month, and we stay there maybe a couple of years. And, she'd come over and collect the money every month. And a dollar was worth more then than ten dollars is now. And I, and the men used to work for ten dollars a month, hundred and twenty dollars a year. Used to hire that a way. And, uh, now you can't get a man for, fifty dollars a month. You paying a man now fifty dollars a month, he don't want to work for it.

Interviewer: *More like fifty dollars a week now a days.*

Fountain Hughes: *[laughs] That's just it exactly. He wants fifty dollars a week and they ain't got no more now than we had then. And we, no more money, but course they bought more stuff and more property and all like that. We didn't have no property. We didn't have no home. We had nowhere or nothing. We didn't have nothing only just, uh, like your cattle, we were just turned out. And uh, get along the best you could. Nobody to look after us. Well, we been slaves all our lives. My mother was a slave, my sisters was slaves, father was a slave.*

Interviewer: *Who was you father a slave for Uncle Fountain?*

Fountain Hughes: He was a slave for B. He belong, he belong to B.

Interviewer: *Didn't he belong to Thomas Jefferson at one time?*

Fountain Hughes: He didn't belong to Thomas Jefferson. My grandfather belong to Thomas Jefferson.

Interviewer: *Oh your grandfather did.*

Fountain Hughes: Yeah. And, uh, my father belong to, uh, B. And, uh, and B. died during the wartime because, he was afraid he'd have to go to war. But, then now, you, and in them days you could hire a substitute to take your place. Well he couldn't get a substitute to take his place so he run away from home. And he took cold. And when he come back, the war was over but he died. And then, uh, if he had lived, couldn't been no good.

The Yankees just come along and, just broke the mill open and hauled all the flour out in the river and broke the store open and throwed all the meat out in the street and throwed all the sugar out. And we, we boys would pick it up and carry it and give it to our missus and massa and young massaers, told we come to be, well I don't know how old. I don't know, to tell you the truth when I think of it today, I don't know how I'm living. None, none of the rest of them that I know of is living. I'm the oldest one that I know that's living. But, still, I'm thankful to the Lord. Now, if, uh, if my massa wanted send me, he never say, you couldn't get a horse and ride. You walk, you know, you walk. And you be barefooted and collapse.

That didn't make no difference. You wasn't no more than a dog to some of them in them days. You wasn't treated as good as they treat dogs now. But still I didn't like to talk about it. Because it makes, makes people feel bad you know. Uh, I, I could say a whole lot I don't like to say. And I won't say a whole lot more.

Interviewer: *Do you remember much about the Civil War?*

Fountain Hughes: No, I don't remember much about it.

Interviewer: *You were a little young then I guess, huh.*

Fountain Hughes: I, uh, I remember when the Yankees come along and took all the good horses and took all the, throwed all the meat and flour and sugar and stuff out in the river and let it go down the river. And they knowed the people wouldn't have nothing to live on, but they done that. And that's the reason why I don't like to talk about it. Them people, and, and if you was cooking anything to eat in there for yourself, and if they, they was hungry, they would go and eat it all up, and we didn't get nothing. They'd just come in and drink up all your milk, milk. Just do as they please. Sometimes they be passing by all night long, walking, muddy, raining. Oh, they had a terrible time. Colored people that's free ought to be awful thankful. And some of them is sorry they are free now. Some of them now would rather be slaves.

Interviewer: *Which had you rather be Uncle Fountain?*

Fountain Hughes: Me? Which I'd rather be ? You know what I'd rather do? If I thought, had any idea, that I'd ever be a slave again, I'd take a gun and just end it all right away. Because you're nothing but a dog. You're not a thing but a dog. Night never comed out, you had nothing to do. Time to cut tobacco, if they want you to cut all night long out in the field, you cut. And if they want you to hang all night long, you hang, hang tobacco. It didn't matter about your tired, being tired. You're afraid to say you're tired. They just, well.

Interviewer: *When, when did you come to Baltimore?*

Fountain Hughes: You know when, you don't remember when Garfield died, do you? When they, when they shot Garfield? No, I don't think you was born.

Interviewer: *I don't think I was then.*

Fountain Hughes: No, you wasn't, Well, I don't remember what year that was myself now, but I know you wasn't born. Well, I come to Baltimore that year anyhow. I don't remember what year it was now myself. But if I laid, if I was laying in the bed I could hav remembered. But uh, I don't reember now.

Interviewer: *But did you go to work for Mr. S. when you came to Baltimore?*

Fountain Hughes: Oh no, no. I work for a man by the name of R. when I first come to Baltimore. I used to, I commence to haul manure for him. The old horses was here then. No elec, and no electric cars, and no cable cars. They were all horse cars. And I used to haul manure, go around to different stables, you know. Why people, everybody had horses for, for their use when I first come here. They had coachmen, and men to drive them around. Didn't have no, automobiles, they hadn't been here so long. And uh, and then they put on a cable car, what they call cable car. Well they run them for a little while, or maybe a couple or three years or four years. Then somebody invented the electric car. And that first run on North Avenue. Well, uh, that run a while and they kep't on inventing and inventing till they got them all, different kinds of cars, you know. It was, uh, horse cars. Wasn't no electric cars at all. Wasn't no, wasn' no big cars like they got now you know. I just can't, I just can't think of, uh, what year it was.

Interviewer: *You're not getting tired are you Uncle Fountain?*

Fountain Hughes: No, no I ain't. I'm just same as at home. Just like I was setting in the house. And uh, see what. I was thinking about oh, now you know how we served the Lord when I come along, a boy?

Interviewer: *How was that?*

Fountain Hughes: We would go to somebody's house. And uh, well we didn't have no houses like they got now, you know. We had these what they call log cabin. And they have one, old colored man maybe one would be there, maybe he'd be as old as I am. And he'd be the preacher. Not as old as I am now, but, he'd be the preacher, and then we all sit down and listen at him talk about the Lord.

Well, he'd say, well I wonder, uh, sometimes you say I wonder if we'll ever be free. Well, some of them would say, well, we going to go ask the Lord to free us. So they'd say, well, we, we going to sing "One Day Shall I Ever Reach Heaven and One Day Shall I Fly." Then they would sing that for about a hour. Then they, next one they'd get up and say let's sing a song, "We Gonna Live on Milk and Honey, Way By and By." They'd, they'd, oh I can hear them singing now but I can't, can't, uh, repeat it like I could in them days. But some day when I'm not hoarse, I could tell you, I could sing it for you, but I'm too hoarse now. And then we'd sing...."I'm Gonna," "I'm A-Gonna Sing Around the Altar." Oh, I, I wish I could, I wish I could sing it for you, "I'm Gonna Sing Around the Altar."

Interviewer: *Well I wish you could too.*

Fountain Hughes: And they, they, well this, someday when you come over here and I'm not hoarse, you get me to come up here and I, I'll sing, I'll try to sing it for you.

Interviewer: *O. K. I'm going to do that.*

Fountain Hughes: This is the. Now, I heard, people here now sing about "Roll Jordan Roll." Well that's a old time, that's what the old people used to sing in old back days.

Interviewer: *Is that "Roll Jordan Roll?"*

Fountain Hughes: Yeah. But they don't sing it like the old people used to sing it in them day. They sing it quite different now. And, and another one they sing, "By and By When the Morning Come." Well they sing that different too. But the old, they're getting the old people's song. I hear them come over the radio. I know them all just as good as they, but they sing them different.

Interviewer: *Have different names to some of them, huh?*

Fountain Hughes: Yes. Well they cut them off shorter and all like that. It's a, if I had my voice, I would sing just one for you so you go in that, but I can't do it on account of my voice. But someday you come over here, you come in, you call me up and let me know and how my voice is.

Ever since I took that medicine from my doctor, well it hurt my voice, now there was a preacher in my house the other night, he live right next door to me, and he played on the piano. And he played something and I sung it for him. And now he wants me to go down to his church next Sunday. I told him, I says, "Now if I go down to your church, I'll not sing nothing. Because if I do I'll get ho, hoarse I can't talk." But he said, "Brother Hughes, I don't care whether you sing or not. I just want you to go down there and let the people see who you are. Let them see what a, what a old people is." I said, "Well uh, Reverend, why I'll be glad to go down with you." So, next Sunday I'm going down to his church if I living, and nothing happen. But if he, if he sing something old, I, I, [laughs].

Interviewer: *Just sing along.*

Fountain Hughes: I feel, I feel the spirit now, but I can't, I got to keep quiet. Now you, do you ever hear this fellow that comes over the radio? I think they call him H. Comes on Sunday night about twelve o'clock, on WFBR?

Interviewer: *No I don't know whether I've ever heard him or not.*

Fountain Hughes: Well I, you turn him on. He comes on a quarter after eleven, on Sunday night. Well, you, you must have heard him cause he says, "Can't uh, can't keep a good man down." So, it makes so much noise, look like everybody ought to hear him. But now when that fellow comes around, I'm laying in the bed, don't you know, I get just so I got to be in that, because it's all old time business.

Interviewer: *Uh um.*

Fountain Hughes: And, uh, somebody don't like it. They says, "I don't like H." I says, "Why?" "Oh," he says, "he make too much noise." I say, "Well, well, the, the Bible say make a noise over Jesus? Jesus said make a noise over me, so he makes a noise over him." And I does enjoy certain of his show.

Oh, he's got a big crowd and we just get so happy I got to do that too. Boy, when you feel the grace of God you've got to jump up. I lay in bed, I got to get up. Why you have to carry on. And then next morning I can't talk. Doctor gave me that medicine, it just tore me all to pieces.

Interviewer: *Uh huh, uh, I see. I sure hope it comes back again because I'd love, I'd like to hear you sing.*

Fountain Hughes: Well old people used to say, "Wonder If I Shall Ever Reach Heaven or Wonder Shall I Fly." I, I used to could sing it. I can sing well sometimes, when I hear the spirit, you know and I may get to singing something again someday. People now.

Interviewer: *Do you go to church every Sunday Uncle Fountain?*

Fountain Hughes: Uh uh. Don't go to church at all. I set and listen to the radio.

Interviewer: *Listen to it on the radio huh.*

Fountain Hughes: Because I'll tell you why I don't go to church.

Interviewer: *You rather not have this on? Hm? You rather not tell me or you rather not have this on when you tell me?*

Fountain Hughes: It don't make any difference. I ain't going to say nothing wrong. I ain't going to. I, I say. **END OF TAPE**

For more of this interview go to: https://www.loc.gov

LIBRARY OF CONGRESS | Everything ∨ | Fountain Hughes

I see dim go dee way

Interview with Alice Gaston, Gee's Bend, Alabama, 1941 The WPA interviewed her and here's what she had to say:

Alice Gaston: We was talking about in the old war time, the old slavery time.

I can remember when, uh, I can remember when the Yankees come through and, uh, they carried my father away and carried away, my si, two sisters and one brother. And, uh, they left me.

And I can remember when my missus used to run in the garden, from the Yankees and tell us if they come, don't tell them where they at. Told, don't tell nobody where they at when they come and they all come and they told me, don't get scared now and tell them where they is, I told them no, we told them no. And uh, when they come and ask for them I told them I didn't know where they was, and they was in the woods. And this was at the house. And my father, when my father left he carried with the,.. he went away with the Yankees, and carried two, two girls and one son, the oldest one.

Carried them with him. And he when with the Yankees. And I can remember that. And uh, my old missus was named Mrs. M., and the massa was name Mr. F. I. Mr. F. I.

Interviewer: *They treat you pretty good?*

Alice Gaston: Yes sir, they treat me nice. They treat me nice as they could treat me. And then after they left, after they died, then I heard, still here and am here until yet. And the white folks all been treating me mighty nice ever since they knowed me. They treating me all now, that knows me, they treating me nice.

I's came up here over here from Mr. Y., from over to and come to Mr.Y.'s place up here. And he kept me there until he, he died, him and his wife. And then I come on then from that, on down here, and I'm here yet. An' they all treating me mighty nice, all the white folks that know me, they treats me nice. And if I want anything, I'll ask for it. I was taught in that a way by my old massa . Don't steal, don't lie, and if you want anything, ask for it. Be honest in what you get.

That was what I was raised up with. And I'm that a way today.

Interviewer: *What's the government been doing for you here?*

Alice Gaston: They been treating me fine. Ever since I been, ever since I been here with the government they treat me nice. I was in a old house down there, took me out the old house and put me up there in a good house where they could take care of me. And I'm in there yet.

I don't find no fault. Give me enough food to eat, give me clothes to wear. They been treating me just as nice as they can. I can't find no fault.

Interviewer: *Pretty, pretty happy then.*

Alice Gaston: Yes sir, yeh.

For more of this interview go to: https://www.loc.gov

LIBRARY OF CONGRESS | Everything ∨ | Alice Gaston | 🔍

A faithful slave is executed by General William Tecumseh Sherman's Union troops. This is the subject of a slave account by Max Dorsey of Chester, South Carolina.

Reportedly, the slave chose death rather than to be disloyal to his master. The story has been told for generations in Blackstock, South Carolina.

As a matter of American history, the Union Army held raiding parties known as "bummers" along the path of soldiers' march to loot, pillage and plunder individual homes and plantations for food and booty.

One such party arrived at the home of a certain Robert Hemphill, three miles northeast of Blackstock. Hemphill was a wealthy, prestigious planter who owned dozens of slaves. When Sherman's troops approached his home, he ran, leaving his slave Burrel to talk with the Unionists.

Then, aged 12, a grandson of Burrel later recounted the tale of his grandfather's encounter with the soldiers. They were convinced that Burrel knew where Hemphill hid his family silverware, other valuables and cash.

In reality, Burrel only knew where the silverware was because Hemphill took all the money had with him before he left. Despite cruel torture, including being tied to a horse and dragged a half-mile, Burrel yielded no information. When all their abuse failed, soldiers took him to the woods where he was hanged from the limb of a blackgum tree and shot multiple times to death.

Years later, members of the Hopewell community raised funds and resources to establish a granite marker on his grave, bearing the inscription, "In Memory of Burrel Hemphill Killed."

Interview with Uncle Bob Ledbetter, in Oil City, Louisiana, 1940, The WPA interviewed him at this time and here is what he had to say:

Interviewer: *What was that you said, uh? uh, Uncle Bob?*

Bob Ledbetter: What about?

Interviewer: *Uh, the recording machine went off I didn't hear you.*

Bob Ledbetter: I said I'm glad got acquainted with you because I believe you is a good man and I want to be with a good man?

Interviewer: *Well, tell, tell me, where were you born Uncle Bob?*

Bob Ledbetter: I was born not far from this place. Up here south, uh, west of here. About five miles.

Interviewer: *And how old are you?*

Bob Ledbetter: Well now uh, I told you about, oh, they say I'm seventy something, two or three. My daddy told me I was uh, nineteen years old on eight, on the eighteenth of December. And that's all I can go by.

Interviewer: *Eighteenth of December when?*

Bob Ledbetter: Well, 1880.

Interviewer: *Yeah. And you, you don't know to figure how much that is, that makes you now?*

Bob Ledbetter: No sir. I' a poor figurer.

Interviewer: *Uh, you told me a story or two about yourself and about your father as we came along. What were they?*

Bob Ledbetter: Well they, mention it so I know what you talking about and I can start it over again I reckon.

Interviewer: *Well, was your father a songster like you?*

Bob Ledbetter: Nothing but old hymns, hymns. He was regular church man.

Interviewer: *Well what kind of songs did you sing when you were young?*

Bob Ledbetter: Well, I didn't, just hollered reels, just fiddle and reels, you know, all the time, my singing.

Interviewer: *Was it, were you a fiddler yourself?*

Bob Ledbetter: No sir, no sir. I couldn't make no music at all.

Interviewer: *Well you could make music with your mouth.*

Bob Ledbetter: Oh yes sir, I could do that. I sure would do that. Everywhere you hears me you hear me singing a song, a reel.

Interviewer: *And out in the field what did you do when you were working?*

way, old Dan Tucker, Come too late to get your supper. I don't remember, I never did sing it.

Interviewer: *Well how, how did you tell me you used to call your sweetheart out at night?*

Bob Ledbetter: Let me see, I'm near forgot what I was to holler, what sort of holler. [Interviewer interrupts]

Interviewer: *And holler.*

Bob Ledbetter: Just tell me one word of it so I'll know what you talking about.

Interviewer: *You said you didn't have any starch or soap.*

Bob Ledbetter: Yeah. [starts to sing] No soap.

Interviewer: *Louder. Sing it louder.*

Bob Ledbetter: No soap, no starch. Nobody, nobody to wash my clothes, nobody to wash my clothes. I hate to sing to anybody. My voice, it, it broke.

Interviewer: *Well uh, didn't you say you used to sing that in the field too?*

Bob Ledbetter: Yeah I sing that in the field too. Yes sir.

Interviewer: *Would your sweetheart be out there in the field?*

Bob Ledbetter: No, she'd be enjoining, enjoying, enjoining fields you know.

Interviewer: *Uh huh. Well what was some of the other old field hollers that you used to have?*

Bob Ledbetter: [starts to sing] I'm going home. I'm going home. I'm going home. That was one of them.

Interviewer: *Well when you wanted to, when you wanted to summon a boy from across the creek way far off, how would you, how would you notify him?*

Bob Ledbetter: I just holler that holler, you hear me a-hollering. And he'd answer me way over yonder.

Interviewer: *Well what was, what was the holler?*

Bob Ledbetter: That same thing I was singing. [starts to sing]

No soap, no starch, Nobody to wash my clothes, nobody to wash my clothes. That same old holler. And he'd answer me way out at his field.

Second Interviewer: *What'd he say?*

Bob Ledbetter: Ma'am?

Interviewer: *What would he say?*

Bob Ledbetter: Well he'd sing the same thing.

Interviewer: *And how would he sing it? Sing it like he did.*

Bob Ledbetter: [starts to sing] No soap, no starch, Nobody to wash my clothes, nobody to wash my clothes. And if he took a notion then he'd say: [sings] I'm going home. I'm going home. I knowed that he's coming soon as he got supper. At the white folk kitchen [laughs] I looking for him.

Interviewer: *Now you told me about the, the man that you worked for, for ten or twelve years.*

Bob Ledbetter: Mr. Norris?

Interviewer: *Yeah, and you said he was the meanest man in the country.*

Bob Ledbetter: Well they said so. Them Norris' would work for the meanest people there was around.

Interviewer: *Well, how'd they treat you?*

Bob Ledbetter: They treat me all right. Nary a one of them never did cuss at me the whole twelve year. And didn't care what I went to them for, I got it. Barrels of flour, middlings of meat, kegs of molasses, money any time. Now that Judge Norris? that was the oldest boy.

And his store would be full of hands you know, and he wouldn't want them all to know what he's doing. I just tell him, give me your pencil and piece of paper. He'd hand it to me and I'd write on there, I'd tell him I want five dollar, please sir. I'd hand it to him and go on about my business. First thing you know he'd come on by me, touch me, and give it to me. He'd do me that-a-way just as sure as he is, just as sure as I'm living.

Interviewer: *Well now what was it the old merchant, what was it the old merchant told you? You told the old merchant down here that ???*

Bob Ledbetter: Uh, Mr. [Interviewer Interrupts]

Interviewer: *Morinfort?*

Bob Ledbetter: Me and him was talking now one day and uh, wasn't nobody in there but me.

Interviewer: *Now say exactly what you said now.*

Bob Ledbetter: Yes sir. Wasn't nobody in there but me and him and his son and his son's daughter. And I say "Mr. C.," I forgot what just exactly how old I was, but anyhow I said, "I'm sixty-one or two years old, and I never had no trouble in my life."

I say "I never ask the Norris' for a nickel, what they didn't give it to me, in my life and nary a one of them never did cuss at me." And say "I ain't never been summoned and ain't never been arrested, and ain't never been to the jail house but twice in my life, and I ain't been to the courthouse but twice." He, he looked at me and he cussed.

He said, "Well, Bob, I be damn if that ain't too much for a nigga to say." Said "there ain't nary a white man can say any better than that." Said, There ain't. I say, Well, I'm telling you the truth, I say, You can ask these people all around Morinfort, that know me, and they'll tell you I ain't never been no trouble since I been there.

Interviewer: *Well you said you hadn't been into the jailhouse but twice. Did they put you in jail twice?*

Bob Ledbetter: No sir, no sir, just went by there.

Interviewer: *Went by the jail.*

Bob Ledbetter: Down the street, yes.

Interviewer: *Well when you had friends in jail, didn't you go see them?*

Bob Ledbetter: I didn't go see them because I always said practice makes perfect. [*laughs*] I was proud I said so, and I just wouldn't go to see them.

I says no I ain't going see them. I said practice makes perfect. I ain't going there. Well Lord knows I'm telling you the truth what I said.

Interviewer: *Uh, uh, how much, how much school did you go to?*

Bob Ledbetter: I never went to school a day in my life, not a hour. Hey, hey, hey, howdy, howdy.

New person enter room: *Is that you?*

Bob Ledbetter: Yeah. How you feel Nora?

Nora: *All right.*

Second Interviewer: *We're gonna have to get some more chairs.*

Bob Ledbetter: *Well Nora here can tell you I never went to school a hour in my life.*

Second Interviewer: *See if I can get you a chair.*

Interviewer: *Well is it still recording, running here?*

Second Interviewer: Yeah.

Bob Ledbetter: Well go ahead. Talk to Nora

Interviewer: *So you never went to ??? .*

Bob Ledbetter: I, I say, she can tell you, I never went to school a hour in my life.

Interviewer: *Uh huh.*

Bob Ledbetter: Not a hour.

Interviewer: *Well, you, you, then could you read and write?*

Bob Ledbetter: I could read and write too. I do, I can send a letter all over this world if I just knowed where to send it. Course I can't write it pretty like people do do, but anywhere I know where to send it, I can send it.

Interviewer: *Well, uh, how did you learn to write?*

Bob Ledbetter: Well my daddy just taught me how to spell a little at night. Well after that then he kept, uh, copies, and I take copies and just learn myself.

Interviewer: *And how you learn to read?*

Bob Ledbetter: Well he learn me at night. He said he, he wasn't no educated man. He could just read printing. And he set up at night and teach his children. That's the way we learned.

Interviewer: *I heard a story about, uh, a judge asking a colored boy on the witness stand, he said, uh, "Jim, can you read writing?"*

He said, "No sir, Judge. I can't even read reading." [all laugh] But you can read reading and writing both.

Bob Ledbetter: Yes sir. They had a, they had a preacher treated us fine. He could make a, uh, preacher out of him. And they ask him could he, did he know, did he know theology.

He said, "No sir, I never knowed that man in my life. I, I never have been acquainted with him." [laughs]

So I don't know, know nothing about no, nothing like that.

Interviewer: *Uh, how old were you when you joined the church?*

Bob Ledbetter: I was, uh, uh, nineteen years old.

Interviewer: *And how old were you when you got married?*

Bob Ledbetter: I was, uh, just, just in my twenty. Just started in my twenties.

Interviewer: *Well did your wife make you join the church?*

Bob Ledbetter: No sir. Just joined myself. Just took a notion and join myself.

Interviewer: *Well how have you got along so well in life? What, what, what, what's been your principles?*

Bob Ledbetter: Well people around, ask the people, anybody you know around here, ask them about my principles. I just went on, just knowed, I just knowed what was right to do and I always try to do what's right.

Interviewer: *Well that's a mighty good way to do Uncle Bob.*

Bob Ledbetter: Yes sir, I know what's right and I tried my best to do what's right in everything I do.

Interviewer: *How many times have you voted?*

Bob Ledbetter: Ain't voted but twice. Vote for whiskey once and voted President election once.

Interviewer: *What President election?*

END OF SIDE A.

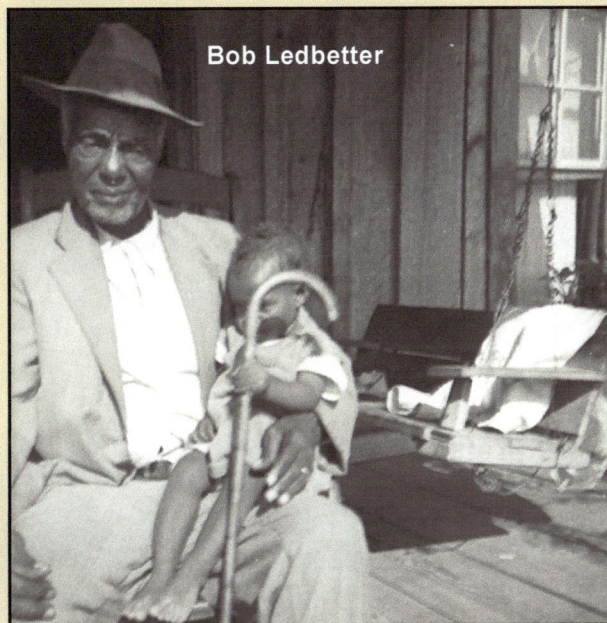

Bob Ledbetter

For more of this interview go to: https://www.loc.gov

LIBRARY OF CONGRESS

Everything ∨	Bob Ledbetter	🔍

Did the election of 1876 lead to the end of Reconstruction?

As a matter of historical fact, it did.

Reconstruction started after the American Civil War between 1865 and 1877. It was a programmatic effort by President Abraham Lincoln and his administration to address inequality caused by slavery and its political, social and economic effects on former black slaves.

Initially called the Ten Percent Plan to refer to voters who swore national loyalty to qualify to establish a state government, Reconstruction was also meant to readmit 11 Southern states that broke away from the Union before or after the war started.

It was also aimed at resolving related longstanding issues facing those states and past secession. Reconstruction succeeded in seeking to rebuild and redirect the socioeconomic lives of former black slaves throughout the Deep South.

The policy brought all Southern states back into the national fold and addressed their most pressing matters. In this era, though to the vehement opposition and eventual setback by whites, African Americans filled the voter rolls for the first time in the country's history.

Then, blacks sought and held elective office at all the city, county, state and federal jurisdictional levels of government, including in both houses of Congress. Still, due to violent repression by Southern whites, much of the objectives of Reconstruction were left unaccomplished.

At this time, the 13th and 14th Amendments of the U.S. Constitution were created but not enforced and stayed on the books. They were to later provide the legal basis for the Civil Rights movement in the 20th century.

As a result, by the time of the election of 1876, voter suppression was rampant throughout the post-Confederacy South.

Hayes would have won the election if it was a fair and peaceful one. However, the electoral process was marked by voter fraud by both parties and crushing the right to vote of African Americans.

In the running at the time were candidates Rutherford B. Hayes, a former Ohio governor and a Republican, and Samuel Tilden, a New Yorker and a Democrat.

Tilden actually won the popular vote but there was a dispute in the Electoral College. Votes in South Carolina, Florida, Louisiana and Oregon were questioned. To resolve the dispute, Congress formed a special committee and tasked it with choosing a winner.

Republican lawmakers hoped to easily promote Hayes and reached across the aisle to Democrat lawmakers. However, the latter refused to allow the former to bring a compromise to a vote.

To pander to the Democrats, who were largely white Southerners, Hayes promised to remove the last vestige of Northern soldiers stationed in Louisiana. This policy became known as the Compromise of 1877.

The troops were originally placed there to oversee and enforce the rights of former slaves against angry, racist whites. The Democrats agreed to this compromise and Hayes won the election. As he promised, the Republicans executed the new act, effectively ending Reconstruction.

Gone were the legal and military protections that allowed African Americans to make use of their newly-won freedom and civil liberties. With the end of Reconstruction, Southerners reclaimed their state governments from Republicans and their territories from the occupation of Northerners.

As a result of the compromise, Southerners now enjoyed what was known as "home rule," which allowed them to legally control their cities, counties and states. An all-powerful, right-wing white supremacist movement evolved throughout the Deep South.

With no federal supervision of southern states overtime, racist, extremist groups such as the Ku Klux Klan emerged and states began to draw up and implement the Jim Crow codes, which continues to shape the political and socioeconomic landscape of the South to this day.

He had a cornstalk fiddle and a cornstalk bow.

Interview with Mr. George Johnson, Mound Bayou, Mississippi, September 1941. The WPA interviewed him and here is what he had to say:

Interviewer: *Oh, ah, you say you, you in AME? [African Methodist Episcopal Church]*

Mr. George Johnson: AME, yes, sir.

Interviewer: *Do you remember how you got religion down there on the ah, plantation?*

Mr. George Johnson: Oh, lord, yes indeed, yeah, yeah, indeed. We just got, just got converted just, right in daytime. Right in the daytime. God spoke peace to our soul, that's in the daytime. Noontime.

It's just noontime. Cause it's called noontime. Eleven o'clock. Yes, sir. Ain't no question about it. We didn't have, I didn't go to no. Just got, got blessed right? come home to and told mom about it.

Interviewer: *Mhmm.*

Mr. George Johnson: And they saw me carried me on to church. And took me to church that same day, same night.

Interviewer: *Well, were they running a meeting?*

Mr. George Johnson: Yes, sir. Yes, sir. Right on Hurricane.

Interviewer: *Mhmm.*

Mr. George Johnson: Right on Hurricane. Right on Jeff Davis plantation.

Interviewer: *Ah you remember who the preacher was?*

Mr. George Johnson: Oh, I know his name better than I know my own name: O. A. Douglass.

Interviewer: *O. A. Douglass?*

Mr. George Johnson: O. A. Douglass, pastor our church.

Interviewer: *Was he a good, good preacher?*

Mr. George Johnson: Yes, sir, Yes, sir.

Interviewer: *Ah what kind of songs did they sing in the church then?*

Mr. George Johnson: Now, ah, well they sing songs like they sing now. Now let me tell you a song we used to sing when I was a boy: Mercy me, the calm and easy Mercy me. See. We sang that song. We sang that song down there when I was a little boy. *[George sings]*

Mercy me. There is a calm, Oh, sure to be. It's under neath the Mercy me. Oh, Mercy me. Oh, Mercy me. Calm to be, Oh, Mercy me. There is a calm, Oh, sure to be. Around a calm, Oh, Mercy me.

Mr. George Johnson: That's one of our favorite songs.

Interviewer: *Mhmm.*

Mr. George Johnson: Yes, sir right in church. And all the women shout: 'My Lord, oh mercy.'

Interviewer: *[laughter]*

Mr. George Johnson: Yes, sir.

Interviewer: *Did they have these things in this church then that they called the shouts?*

Mr. George Johnson: Shouts? Yes, sir. Yes, sir. They shout without end.

Interviewer: *Well, I don't mean when they, when they ju, ju, jump up and shout, but these, these kind of singing they called the shouts, then?*

Mr. George Johnson: No, sir. I don't think we did. No, sir. Not in my day.

Interviewer: *Di, did they have any Baptist on your plantation?*

Mr. George Johnson: Yes, sir. We had plenty Baptist. Plenty Baptist. Main church we had there Baptist Church.

Interviewer: *Di, did they do any different singing and things from what you all did?*

Mr. George Johnson: Mighty little. Mighty little.

Interviewer: *You all sang about the same things they did?*

Mr. George Johnson: Yes, sir. They all was well reckon they Christianized, you understand, under they pastor and our pastor, you understand, they all sang together. They mixed. You couldn't hardly find tell the difference, you know. Cause they all mixed together. Go to one church. Go to the other, see.

Interviewer: *Mhmm.*

Mr. George Johnson: They all? They all Christianized. Yes, sir. All Christianized. Charles S. Johnson: Well ah, di,di,did you all have any ah, did, did, did, did, did you remember any of the Negroes singing in the fields? Any s- songs out there? Any songs out there, liked to sing when they were out in the fields?

Mr. George Johnson: In the fields? I hear them, I used hear them singing Old Black Joe, in the fields.

Interviewer: *You did?*

Mr. George Johnson: Yes, sir. When I was quite a boy I sing, Old Black Joe. Remember that song used o sing:

Old Black Joe Gone am the days when my heart was young and gay. Gone am the friend from a cotton field away. Gone from this world to a better world I know. I hears a voice a calling, Old Black Joe. I am coming keep a coming. From I am a voice a calling, Old Black Joe.

Mr. George Johnson: Yeah, you see that's how men sing out in the field. Yes, sir.

Interviewer: *Di, did they sing any reels?*

Mr. George Johnson: Well, I don't know that much. I ain't hear but. Most things I hear them, I hear at down pretty far from where I lived, you understand. Right around here, they didn't sing no tough songs, you understand, around, near the house. You understand. See cause still Missile Hill.

Interviewer: *Still Missile Hill tough song.*

Mr. George Johnson: Yeah, Missile Hill. Yes tough song, they wouldn't sing that around the house.

Interviewer: *Mhmm*

Mr. George Johnson: But I always down in massa Jeff's yard, you understand. Down in Grandpa's shop. And ah, they wouldn't? mighty nice down there? Yes, sir.

Interviewer: *Well, where did you first hear the blues?*

Mr. George Johnson: After I come up here.

Interviewer: *After you came up here to Mound Bayou?*

Mr. George Johnson: Yes. Yes, sir. Yes, sir.

Interviewer: *Well, what do you think about the blues? Do you think they're good music, eh?*

Mr. George Johnson: Well, I don't, I don't like it.

Interviewer: *You don't like the blues?*

Mr. George Johnson: Don't like the blues. It's too wild for me. I'm scared of it.

Interviewer: *It's too wild?*

Mr. George Johnson: Too wild. Hear it when come up here. Yes, sir. Yes, sir.

Interviewer: *Well, in the song, in the ah, in the dances that that you all had up here, you all didn't play any of that kind of music for your dances?*

Mr. George Johnson: No, sir. No. We played. We played now this here, we play up here now, this Ragtime stuff they play now, why, that's today's stuff, you understand. That's modern dance, you understand. See.

Interviewer: *Mhmm.*

Mr. George Johnson: Now we be dancing four-teen on a set.

Interviewer: *Mhmm.*

Mr. George Johnson: Yeah, four over there. Four over there. Four here and four there. And they all dance. They call Swing, you understand. Part as you swing.

Interviewer: *Mhmm.*

Mr. George Johnson: Meet your partners, like that, you understand. See. Part as you swing. Dance to your partner. Dance to your right. Dance to your left. Then on to your partner. Then on to the other fellow, you understand, see.

Interviewer: *Mhmm.*

Mr. George Johnson: And then get, bring pull into your partner. Your partner pull you back. Then pull back to your partner again. Then half swing around. Half swing around. Till you got to the bar then point her to the bar.

Interviewer: *Mhmm.*

Mr. George Johnson: That, that's the dance we had then. Yes, sir.

Interviewer: *Did you ever play any for the white people's dances?*

Mr. George Johnson: Down there?

Interviewer: *Mhmm.*

Mr. George Johnson: Played music. Brass band for them.

Interviewer: *That's what I mean.*

Mr. George Johnson: Yes, sir. Played string band for white folks. Brass band.

Interviewer: *Wha, what, what kind of, what kind of music di, di, did they have? They have the same you had, or did they have different songs you played for them?*

Mr. George Johnson: Naw, they we, we played just the string band. Me and the brass band played for white folk. They'd have a big outing, you understand. In their lawn. We played music for them you understand. Brass band music, you know.

Interviewer: *Mhmm.*

Mr. George Johnson: They'd have people up there dancing. Didn't somebody wouldn't have a dance like the way we have. They just dance, you understand, their way.

Interviewer: *Mhmm.*

Mr. George Johnson: But we played that brass band music, you understand. You see.

Interviewer: *Mhmm.*

Mr. George Johnson: Yes, sir. We played in that square front of Joe Davis' house. Right in the shade. Right in the great big shade. Right in Joe Davis' ya, yard. Yard big as the railroad over there.

Interviewer: *Mhmm.*

Mr. George Johnson: Yes, sir. Like, massa Jeff's yard was. Yes, sir.

Interviewer: *Well ah, you didn't like these songs like ah, Joe Turner: Make Me A Pallet On the Floor?*

Mr. George Johnson: No, sir. I didn't like those kind things. No, sir. No, sir. I hear a guy that come up here. Yes, sir.

Interviewer: *Ah what year was that? Ah what year did you first hear there? About what time was it.*

Mr. George Johnson: Oh, been about fifty-years ago.

Interviewer: *Mhmm.*

Mr. George Johnson: Since I been here.

Interviewer: *Mhmm.*

Mr. George Johnson: I been here fifty-four years, going on fifty-five.

Interviewer: *Mhmm.*

Mr. George Johnson: I didn't know anything about it since I come up here.

Interviewer: *Mhmm.*

Mr. George Johnson: Yes, sir. They got the lake stuff, come up out of the lake Negro, you understand, see. And he wild. He just say anything.

Interviewer: *[laugh] Say anything.*

Mr. George Johnson: Say anything. He wild. Don't have any culture. Hard to educate, educate him in a way, but in a way he ain't educated. But what he got to do is learn to get his self culture, he won't think he's a little smart.

Interviewer: *Mhmm.*

Mr. George Johnson: Sure he'll do it. Get his self culture. He won't get him a little schooling. He won't do it. Some fellows say, "Well, he'll do so and so," but he ain't used to doing that. Christ said,'Lift me up.' Say, 'If I am lifted it's all men.' Lift them up. That's all men can lift himself up. That' he got do.

This man don't want to do his self like he ain't much. He going be just down there all, down there all the time. He don't care to being raggedy no, no other men?

Interviewer: *Ah did they ever sing the hallee, the hallees, the jubilee songs in the AME Church? They sing a lot of them, used to sing a lot of them in the Baptist Church.*

Mr. George Johnson: Yeah, yeah they did sing them sometime. Sing them. They sing them. They sing them.

Interviewer: *Did you like them?*

Mr. George Johnson: Yes. Yes. they were all, they were all, all they all right.

Interviewer: *Mhmm.*

Mr. George Johnson: We had a preacher in our church, ??? . His name, S. C. Johnson. He could sing world, he could sing how a goat sing. Hollering.

Interviewer: *Mhmm.*

Mr. George Johnson: He could sing without end. He just sing. Then he could preach.

Interviewer: *Mhmm.*

Mr. George Johnson: He could preach. He had a song he used to sing. Say, "The apostle of God, whose salvation he give onto them who love them." His son, he would, he, his son. I remember that song:

Hallelujah Tis Done Hallelujah it's done. I believe on the son. I am saved by the blood of the crucified one. Though the pathway be lonely. And dangerous truth.

Surely Jesus is able to carry me through. Hallelujah it is done. I believe on the son. I am saved by the blood of the crucified one.

Mr. George Johnson: That man could sing that song.

Interviewer: *Mhmm.*

Mr. George Johnson: He could sing it. The whole church understand. You see.

Interviewer: *Mhmm.*

Mr. George Johnson: *Yes, sir.*

Interviewer: *Well ah, ah, how do you like the Dr. Watts songs, these long meter things?*

Mr. George Johnson: Long meters? Well, I didn't care much about them. But I got to hear them. But I never, I never could sing them.

Interviewer: *Never could sing them.*

Mr. George Johnson: Never could sing them. No, sir. Yeah, I heard Dr. Watts' songs lots of times, never could sing them. I had a quick in, in speech. And singing and all that kind of stuff. I learned quick, you understand.

Interviewer: *Mhmm.*

Mr. George Johnson: Then I'm part, I'm Creole.

Interviewer: *Mhmm.*

Mr. George Johnson: I'm part Creole. My father was Virginian. but my mother was from down in Louisiana. Down in, on in a cane farm.

Interviewer: *Mhmm.*

Mr. George Johnson: Place the other side of a New, part of New Orleans there. New Orleans there. Born on the Louisiana side. I can't remember that place now. Her and her brother and my aunty, but my father's from Richmond. My father and my grandfather are from Richmond. My father's brother, uncle Charlie.

Interviewer: *Well, did you all sing anything like ah, ah Swing Low Sweet Chariot and ah—*

Mr. George Johnson: Yeah, we sing that too. We sing that too.

Interviewer: *Did, di, you did you sing that in your church, or did you learn that.*

Mr. George Johnson: Sing that in church.

Interviewer: *From outside?*

Mr. George Johnson: Sing that in church.

Interviewer: *Mhmm.*

Mr. George Johnson: Sing that in church. Right in the church. Right down in church at home old Bethel Church. Sing it with our pastor, O. A. Douglass. Lil, little pastor about my size but your color.

Interviewer: *Well, where there, where there any songs like these spiritual and jubilee songs that they don't sing anymore, that they used to sing when you were, a long time ago?*

Mr. George Johnson: Well, these special songs. They sing them in the revival, you understand. You see.

Interviewer: *Mhmm*

Mr. George Johnson: Those special songs they sing in the revival. But after the revival, why, they something else, you know.

Interviewer: *Mhmm.*

Mr. George Johnson: Yes, sir.

Interviewer: *Well ah, do you remember what you favorite revival song was?*

Mr. George Johnson: Well, I never had no favorite, just the ah older fellows had the, you know favorites, you understand. Like my uncle and all them old folks, you understand. They was leading the young folks, you understand.

Interviewer: *Mhmm.*

Mr. George Johnson: They'd take they message, you understand, and we'd go behind them, you know. You see. Let them lead us and we, we follow.

Interviewer: *Did ah, did your uncle have a song that ah, everybody thought they really liked to hear him sing?*

Mr. George Johnson: No. He never sing it. He, he always sung, he sang the same song about Me and My God, all he sing.

Interviewer: Is that all?

Mr. George Johnson: Yes, sir. All he sing. He liked it.

Interviewer: *Mhmm.*

Mr. George Johnson: My uncle.

Interviewer: *But, but he, he didn't have one of the jubilees ah.*

Mr. George Johnson: No, sir. No, sir.

Interviewer: *Nothing like that he liked.*

Mr. George Johnson: No, sir. Nothing like that. He only sing, Me and My God To Be . I heard him, he sung it all the time. Wonderful fellow too.

Interviewer: *Well where there any famous fiddlers around here when you came?*

Mr. George Johnson: Fiddlers? Let me see. We had a, we had a fellow here,.. man, you ask me about a fiddler?

Interviewer: *Mhmm.*

Mr. George Johnson: We had it after I was a boy down home. We had a fiddler down home there. We had a fiddler down home there named, Ed Phillips. He'd play that fiddle all night. Had a man pick a banjo, name ah, name Old Man Ed Green. And ah I think about a piece they used, used to play. He'd sing a song, you understand, his song but for his piece he used to play, you understand, say: I Lost my fiddle and lost my bow. Am glad I don't have go home and play no more.

[both men erupt in laughter] And he had a cornstalk fiddle and a cornstalk bow. And never play no more. And he'd sing that song and play them fiddle and that banjo without end. Man name, Ed Phillips. Never forget his name. He lived right on the lake right across from Mound Brierfield Place. Right across, about three mile.

Interviewer: *Mhmm.*

Mr. George Johnson: Somewhere by it over there at Lickfield Place, you understand. All that belonged to massa Jeff, understand. That's his. All that land. And ah, they come over there and hear them cords and they'd play all night. They play all night. Just dance like three little old boys. Yes, sir.

Interviewer: *Well, do you remember anything else they played besides from, I Lost My Fiddle and I Lost My Bow?*

Mr. George Johnson: No. Naw, I'm a have to think about it.

Interviewer: *Well did, well, did ah the children around the quarters have any games that they liked to play? That they sang to?*

Mr. George Johnson: No. They, they always played ball and played marbles. And played monpeg.

Interviewer: *Mhmm.*

Mr. George Johnson: See them chase it's night, you understand; see them going play monpeg you understand. And they playing marbles. And playing baseball. They had no other games play.

Interviewer: *But, but little children didn't play any jumping games—*

Mr. George Johnson: No, sir.

Interviewer: *—and singing games?*

Mr. George Johnson: Nothing like that. No, sir. No, sir. We ain't had nothing like that. Then what we learned, you understand, we learned from children from Vicksburg. Children from Vicksburg, come down here excursions, you understand. Changed our children how to do things, you understand.

Interviewer: *Mhmm.*

Mr. George Johnson: They learned how to play croquette, so on like that. And learned them how to play dominoes.

Interviewer: *Mhmm.*

Mr. George Johnson: Showed them everything I was a boy. The children from Vicksburg come there on steamboats. They take our children, they all get in a gang, they all in there playing dominoes. Playing croquette and all like that, you know.

Interviewer: *They used to come, they used to come on excursions from Vicksburg—*

Mr. George Johnson: Yes, sir.

Interviewer: *—to Davis Bend?*

Mr. George Johnson: Davis Bend. The white people come down there in their hacks on steamboats just to see massa Jeff's plantation, you understand. And drive them guest all around, all the plantations see them niggas farm.

Interviewer: *Mhmm.*

Mr. George Johnson: On massa Jeff's place. All the plantations.

Interviewer: *And to bring some of the colored people out.*

Mr. George Johnson: Yes, sir. From the river. And they, people come up there all the way from Natchez up to Bend. Do the same thing. Come all around on the Bend and see mater Jeff's plantation. Everybody come to see. Everybody.

Interviewer: *Well.*

For more of this interview go to: https://www.loc.gov

Many unfamiliar with the real history of black fiddling don't know that it was extremely common among African Americans until the early 20th century.

Multiple historical accounts abound of Africans in America fiddling and making fiddles almost as soon as they arrived from the continent.

The excellence of Black fiddlers performing both for white masters, patrons and paying audience and for the dances and parties of other Africans in America, speaks to the training in European violin playing some slaves received.

It also reflects the musical traditions involving the use of African bowed instruments that slaves brought here. No wonder, fiddling was the most widely reported category of musical performance of African Americans during colonial times.

From the early 1700s to the Civil War, enslaved and free black fiddlers performed music for dances and house parties hosted by elite plantation owners at their farms and townhouses in the American South.

For the black community, the fiddlers played a very different role. Black fiddlers combined the European dance music they performed at high-visibility white social events with ballads, church hymns, African melodies and rhythms and their Caribbean variations to create a distinctive fusion music that served to bind together black diaspora experience in the American South.

In their music, we hear the soundtrack of slavery. When black fiddlers moved west and north in the 1800s, their soundtrack gained crossover appeal, becoming so attractive and popular that, after the Civil War, it was mainstreamed and diluted.

But it has not been lost. Early black fiddler traditions have been passed down from one generation to the next.

Some early black fiddler music has been revived, most notably by the Carolina Chocolate Drops, a Grammy Award-winning, "old-timey music" string quartet from Durham, North Carolina.

Some of the best resources for information is the Depression-era WPA files at the Mississippi Department of Archives and History, which houses numerous interviews and other documents rooted in fieldwork.

In the early part of the nation's history, slave musicians played fiddle music to entertain themselves or their masters. Fiddles were made in any shape and from any wood box that could act as a resonating chamber. The earliest slave banjos and fiddles were constructed from gourds. The finest violin is, after all, simply a very carefully constructed wooden box.

The most important aspect of the fiddle was its ability to project a sound so a musician could learn or practice or even play for dances and other social events.

The devil played an important role in developing scholarship among Delta blues musicians because many blues artists entered the recording industry to rebel against their local preachers or Protestant ministers who warned against music as a corrupting force.

Preachers or ministers called the fiddle "the Devil's box" because some thought it was sinful to play one. In some instances in recent years, visitors to old log cabins in different parts of the Deep South would tear them down to get at the logs and to find old beat-up fiddles hidden in the walls.

At first, these visitors were puzzled over this but local residents explained that a man who lived there was once a fine, old-time fiddler, but, in later years, he had "gotten religion."

In his zeal, the man in question became convinced that he must turn his old life around, and, especially, that devil's instrument, the fiddle!

I can recollect just as good.

Order prints at: newsonpublishing.com/product/wish-i-had-coffee/

Interview with Uncle Billy McCrea, Jasper, Texas, 1940, The WPA interviewed him and here's what he had to say to us:

Interviewer 1: *What do you remember about when slavery was over?*

Uncle Billy McCrea: When slavery was over, let me see if I can't tell you about that.

Interviewer 1: *Well you said you, they all kept going, tell be about them coming through here with cannons.*

Uncle Billy McCrea: Yes, yes. Now I'll tell you when slavery, way back in slavery time, I was standing at [Pointing with his finger] , that's when the Negro was freed. I would, we all would go out every day, right here in town, to see the Yankees all going back home. I can recollect just as good. They'd just have six and eight mules to a cannon, going through and bolted to them there, uh, uh cannons.

Then they'd take the wagon they had bolts all them wagons. Then walk, nothing but them mules, and one man a-riding, riding two mules, we all use to take a look at them.

You understand? All day long be crossing, I remember just as well, and all the Yankees I recollect was blue, was dressed in blue clothes, I can remember it, with blue junk right here, and [Pointing with his finger] had a little pin on, on the coat right there. In fact I'm, and course it was up here. You, yeah, I recollect just as well, day they come around, and they, black mules, have uh, maybe, oh I don't know how many black horses. Men they come along in with lot of these old gray mules, on it, hitched to them cannons.

And then they come back with sorrel horses. That way for two days, they was going out through Jasper, two day. And I remember and the Yankees stop here, and the Yankees stop right here on the courthouse square. I was a good size boy then. And then what they call Freedman Bureau, you hear tell of it ain't you? And they prosecuting people you know, for what they do, you know, and all like that, and I mean just as hard as they could. I've seen two mens they had they were punishing for what they do. And I see them just take them. In uh, a big tent. We, we boys would go out and see them, and they'd take them, hang them up by his thumb. And just let that hang out, so many men, then let him down. That's the punishment they got.

I recollect an old man that they had in town, an old dep, uh, sheriff. His name was

36

Yankee White. And the man, the judge's name, I forgot his name. But anyhow I know you recollect Yankee White. That's when you was young. Well then they come, and my old massa , old Col. M. he bought one, two of the horses from him.

I recollect, I rode the horse a many a time. One of those big horse they call Yankee Tom, big sorrel horse. And another big old horse was a saddle horse, old Col. M.bought, and he was called Boston. He was a great big black horse. Now he took them all down to the farm, I recollect all of that. I was a big, big boy then. A good big boy. And the Yankees had come, and after a while there'd be a whole troop of men come, they said they was Yankees. All walking, all walking. That crew of Yankees would go through. Next time you see, there come a whole troop of Yankees, all riding horses, big guns a-hanging on in there, and all like that you know. Yeah.

We all would stand looking at them, all going home. And I said, I ask them, I said, I ask them, I say, where they, where they going?" said, "They all going home now." And old Col. M. that was our massa , he was in there, and he say, "Well, Harriet, all of you niggas is all free now.

Yankees all going home." I remember that just as well. Right, right in town where we living at. Right above the new Post Office. That was my old, old massa's home, right, uh, up, above the old new Post Office. Well that is his square, from that Post Office clean down to the Citizen Bank. All that was his whole square there.

And clean over to the old parts, coming on up to toward the Methodist Church. That was my old massa's place. I can remember he was a speculator. I can remember it, I was good big boy then. He had a big old shed there. And he, and he had cotton all in that shed, and we boys would all go up and play in that shed everyday. And he had, a, had wagon, every, everyday he'd load up all them wagon and take all that cotton and go off, go off. Now you see, that, that was in slavery times. I recollect just as well, and he'd bring back whole lot of the colored people. Old Col. M., they said he was a speculator.

And he sell them to all these people around this country. There's lot of old people, they all dead now, what he brought there and sold. He'd go off and bring them in. I recall that my old papa was his wagoner. I used to go, he used to carry me with him all the time. Used to haul cotton, carry cotton from Jasper to Wise's Bluff. And, and carry it to Wise's Bluff, and they'd carry cotton over here and weigh it up at a place they call uh, forgot that place now. Carry cotton. I remember he used to be, he used to always be working. I was good, big boy at the time, and he had a oxen, had a old oxen name Brandy.

That how i become he wagoner. He'd get tired and sit down. "Bill." "Yes sir." "Get on, that, get this whip and get on it." And I'd ride old Brandy. Ride old Brandy, drive the rest of them. Ride him, till I get tired and get down, then walk side of them. I been, I own it, I been through a heap [laughs] all that stuff. That, that was in slavery time, that was old slavery time, it was. And I remember I can tell you some more about slavery time. Right down, right down close to Mississippi, uh, M.'s place there was an old jail house there, old log jail house was there. That, that's only, that's all, that's the way, and wasn't no, wasn't no court, wasn't no, or some king of courthouse, I recollect it. And used to put prisoners in that jailhouse. And me, and another young white fellow I believe his name C. M., And we used to go home to people that worked in the kitchen.

We used to go home and steal bread and stuff and poke it through them little bars

to the prisoners. We was boys. That's right here in Jasper. And it was an old log jailhouse. And all around, And I recollect one time, we all was looking at it. And they brought in hounds with three niggas with them hound, runaway niggas, you know, caught in the wood. And they, right, right across, right at the creek there, they take them niggas and put them on, and put them on a log lay them down and fasten them. And whup them. You hear them niggas hollering and praying on them logs. And there was a nigga that bring them in. Then they take them out down there and put them in jail.

Interviewer 1: *That'll be enough. [slight pause]*

Uncle Billy McCrea: Now I see all of that when I was a boy.

Second part of Interview with Uncle Billy McCrea.

Interviewer 1: Introducing to *Miss Sarah, "This is Uncle Billy McCrea".*

Interviewer Miss Sarah: *How ya doing Uncle Billy? How are you this evening?*

Uncle Billy McCrea: I'm feeling very well ??? .

Interviewer Miss Sarah: *Have a seat?*

Interviewer 1: *Uncle Billy, come sit right here and let's, oh, you want sit.*

Interviewer Miss Sarah: *I think maybe he—*

Interviewer 1: *Right over there. Sit in that.*

Uncle Billy McCrea: Yes, sir.

Interviewer 1: *And I want sit over here by you and talk to you some.*

Uncle Billy McCrea: This always?

Interviewer Miss Sarah: *Rest your hat down there. That right. Rest your hat down there.*

Uncle Billy McCrea: I didn't want come, my voice is not good. I can't, I'm afraid I can't do what I, talk like I wanna talk.

Interviewer Miss Sarah: *Well, that'll be fine. We.*

Uncle Billy McCrea: [*Grunts*]

Interviewer Miss Sarah: *Get along fine.*

Interviewer 1: *If you don't sing, Mr Billy, please you tonight I'll, we'll bring you back in the daytime.*

Uncle Billy McCrea: Sir?

Interviewer 1: *If you're not satisfied with them tonight, well I'll bring you back in the daytime, when you're feeling better.*

Uncle Billy McCrea: Yes, sir.

Interviewer 1: Now go head and, ah sing one of those steamboat songs.

Uncle Billy McCrea: You want hear one of those steamboat songs?

Interviewer 1: *Yep.*

Uncle Billy McCrea: I'm just not steady now. I don't wanna start then. They want me to sing that song sort of like.

Interviewer 1: *Blow Cornie Blow.*

Uncle Billy McCrea: You want me sing that song like before they going to work.

Interviewer 1: *Yeah.*

Uncle Billy McCrea: Yeah. Well. I'll sing like going to work. I'll sing it for you.

Interviewer 1: *Go head. Nothing here gonna hurt you.*

Uncle Billy McCrea: [Sing]

Blow Cornie Blow I think I hear a the captain call me blow cornie blow. I think I hear the captain calling blow cornie blow. A blow cornie blow. Blow cornie blow. A blew it cold, loud and mournful. Blow cornie blow.

I think I hear the captain? blow cornie blow. They carried lo-o-o-o-ong onto bend. Blow cornie blow. They soon will be to the landing corner. Blow cornie blow. De captain hand me down my salary. Blow cornie blow. Oh, blow boy and let them hear you. Blow cornie blow. Oh, blow loud and Blow cornie blow. Oh, blow loud just so he can hear you. Blow cornie blow. I think I hear the captain call you. Blow cornie blow.

Uncle Billy McCrea: Yeah. That's the best I.

Interviewer 1: *Now, what were the boys doing when they were singing that?*

Uncle Billy McCrea: What you doing?

Interviewer 1: *Yeah.*

Uncle Billy McCrea: Toting salt.

Interviewer 1: *Toting salt?*

Uncle Billy McCrea: Yes, sir.

Interviewer 1: *Where from the boat to the bank?*

Uncle Billy McCrea: From the boat goes back to the warehouse.

Interviewer 1: *Where that salt come from?*

Uncle Billy McCrea: I don't know where it come from. We used, we got, they got it for old massa .

Interviewer 1: *Yeah.*

Uncle Billy McCrea: Old massa just sit beside you know and they ah, when they land now, then you had to tote it up this bank and put it in the warehouse. And they would sing the while they's toting it.

Interviewer 1: *Well now they'd sing Handy Gal also, wouldn't they?*

Uncle Billy McCrea: No. This here's another one.

Interviewer 1: *All right.*

Uncle Billy McCrea: Let's see here how's that go. We used to just tear that up. Now I sung them you see.

Interviewer 1: *Oh, Sally, What Ya Gonna Have For Dinner? was that one of them?*

Uncle Billy McCrea: That's one of them.

Interviewer 1: *Well, sing that one.*

Uncle Billy McCrea: Let's see now how that go. I got to study it a while. That's the reason why I didn't even, didn't want come cause I done have it preach now see, I tell you how this. Let, I need to talk a little bit. You see here? Why yes. See, I had to run here for two years, and, and not going, and you hurt me. It seem like it's aged my voice. But you don't hurt me on just this time. Well, now I see, let me see how that go?

Interviewer 1: *How about the [Jerah Rall (?)] Don't Come To My House?*

Uncle Billy McCrea: Yeah. That's a good one too.

Interviewer 1: *Alright. Sing in that one.*

Uncle Billy McCrea: [sings]

Ju Rawsy Row, Row, Don't Come To My House Ju rawsy raw, raw, don't come to my house. Ju rawsy raw, raw, don't come to my house. Ju rawsy raw, raw, hoe, hoe. Ju rawsy raw, raw, hoe nigga hoe. Ju rawsy raw, raw, hoe nigga hoe. Ju rawsy raw, raw, a good dog. Ju rawsy raw, raw, Ju rawsy raw, raw, they frighten me. Ju rawsy raw, raw, old ties could bake your bread. Ju rawsy raw, raw? Old ties a good dog. Ju rawsy raw, raw, old ties a horse?

Ju rawsy raw, raw, tote boy. Tote boy. Ju rawsy raw, raw. Ju rawsy raw, raw, ju rawsy raw. Ju rawsy raw, raw, old ties a good dog. Ju rawsy raw, raw. Ju rawsy raw, raw, tide them old ties up. Ju rawsy raw, raw, take them old ties up. Ju rawsy raw, raw, to go. Ju rawsy raw, raw, old ties tend the crop. Ju rawsy raw, raw, old ties tend the crop. Ju rawsy raw, raw, old ties to bake your bread. Ju rawsy raw, raw, old ties a good dog. Ju rawsy raw, raw, ju rawsy raw, raw. Ju rawsy raw, raw, s'ick them old ties up. Ju rawsy raw, raw, cut them old ties up. Ju rawsy raw, raw, cut them old ties up. Ju rawsy raw, raw.

[Hand drumming] Ju rawsy raw, raw. [drumming] Ju rawsy raw, raw, old ties a biting dog?. Ju rawsy raw, raw, old ties will bite you?. Ju rawsy raw, raw, old ties will hurt you?. Ju rawsy raw, raw old ties a good dog?. Ju rawsy raw, raw, s'ick them old ties up? Ju rawsy raw, raw, cut them old ties up?. Ju rawsy raw, raw, hold them ties up? Ju rawsy raw, raw.

Uncle Billy McCrea: How you like that?

Interviewer 1: *I'd say that's a good one.*

Uncle Billy McCrea: [laughs]

Interviewer 1: *Now, well now, hold up. Ah, go on. Let's finish with those, ah, how about that one Walk Darley. How did that one go?*

Uncle Billy McCrea: Which?

Interviewer 1: *Walk Darley, you said, or, Dooley or something like.*

Uncle Billy McCrea: [sings]

Walk Dooley. Walk Dooley. Walk dooley. Dooley's a good. Do walk a dooley. Dooley's my honey girl. Do raz. Walk dooley. Walking and a talking. Walk dooley. Walking and a talk. Walk dooley, dooley's a hand gal. Dooley.

Uncle Billy McCrea: Let me see. I got that wrong. That's why you don't want my mind don't process nothing. Let me see now. Let me see how I can get that started again. Nope. Cause? That's it.

Let's see, now. [he attempts to sing and [Interviewer Miss Sarah comments about something] Ahha. I got it wrong.

Uncle Billy McCrea, [Resumes song]

Walk dooley. Walk, talk and dooley. Walk dooley. Walk, talk, dooley. Walk dooley. Dooley is a⬚ Walk dooley.

Oh, dooley. Do walk. Dooley. Oh, dooley. Walk dooley. Walk them and a talking. Walk dooley. Walk them and a talk. Do raz. Araz-raz, dooley. Walk dooley, dooley. Do raz. Araz-raz, hoe nigga. Hoe man. Do raz, Walk dooley, hoe down nigga. Walk dooley, I am a good man. Walk dooley, I can do. Walk dooley, walk, talk dooley.

Walk dooley, run along dooley. Walk dooley, talk long dooley. Walk dooley, stepping on dooley. Walk dooley, dooley is a good thing. Walk dooley, dooley let the hogs out. Walk dooley, hoe nigga hoe me. Walk dooley, hoe nigga hoe me.

Do raza I am? Do raza I could pull two men. Do raza I could handle three men. Walk dooley, I could whoop five men. Walk dooley, dooley she's a good gal. Walk dooley, I could slap her husband. Walk I slap Julia. Walk sometime I slap Julia. Walk sometime I slap her jaw. Walk Julia is a good gal. Walk when I slap Julia on the jaw. Walk then she come to be a good girl. Walk Julie.

Uncle Billy McCrea: [Laugh] I got, now, now let me see now?.

Interviewer 1: *Handy Gal.*

Uncle Billy McCrea: Handy Gal. Let me see how it is. [he attempts to sing] Handy Gal . Handy gal. Handyeeee. Handy gal. Handyeeee. Let me see. Handy gal. Handy. Let me see. Handy gal. Let me see. Walk. Handy gal. Let's see. Handy gal. See, I've got to study it. You see. I've got to get to study it, before I could sing it.

Interviewer 1: *That's all right. Ah, oh what about ta.*

Uncle Billy McCrea: Let me see how it is. How that, that song is. That's one of those songs on the boat I was just talking about.

Interviewer 1: *Yeah.*

Uncle Billy McCrea: I don't know what's going happen here.

Interviewer 1: *Yeah.*

Uncle Billy McCrea: Let's see. [he sings one note Oh.] Let's see. How's that go. I had that down good today. Because I told them, I remember sort of leaving. See. [sings] Ohhhh leave won't you ?

Told you I come around here and go, go, go, go sunny your horse is gonna had a good stable. Let's see, carry on?

Interviewer 1: *What did you do on the boats? Ah, ah Uncle Billy?*

Uncle Billy McCrea: Cook. I cooked.

Interviewer 1: *How long?*

Uncle Billy McCrea: On the boat?

Interviewer 1: *Yeah.*

Uncle Billy McCrea: I cooked on boats about six years.

Interviewer 1: *And where did the boats run?*

Uncle Billy McCrea: From Beaumont to Jasper here Gulfport.

Interviewer 1: *How many miles was that?*

Uncle Billy McCrea: N-nnn, I think they taught us, fifty-miles, from Jasper to Beaumont. I cooked on. I cooked on about, cooked for about six years on steamboats.

Interviewer 1: *And how old are you Uncle Billy?*

Uncle Billy McCrea: Well I.

Interviewer 1: *Sit over a little bit.*

Uncle Billy McCrea: Could tell you my age. Now I, I don't rightly know my age. But I can tell you what I go for. The fifteenth of this, of October, I be eighty-nine. Eighty-nine-years-old. And on the second time, the way they've got my age fixed there on the fifteenth I will be a hundred-and seventeen-years-old. But I register in the courthouse, of my age be ninety-eight, ah eight, no eighty nine, this coming, the fifteenth of this month. Next October.

Interviewer 1: *How many children have you, Uncle?*

Uncle Billy McCrea: How many children? I have two children. I, how many children? Let's see. Thirty-six.

Interviewer 1: *Thirty-six?*

Uncle Billy McCrea:

For more of this interview go to: https://www.loc.gov

**LIBRARY
OF CONGRESS**

| Everything ⌄ | Uncle Billy McCrea 🔍 |

In the 1860s, the Emancipation Proclamation by President Abraham Lincoln and the 13th Amendment combined freed all slaves in the United States.

The 14th Amendment acknowledged the citizenship of all freed slaves. Both amendments eventually formed the basis for the Civil Rights Movement of the 1960s.

As a result of this executive order and two legal amendments to the U.S. Constitution, hundreds of thousands of African Americans in the South faced new difficulties: finding a way to forge an economically independent life in the face of hostile whites, little or no education, and few other resources, such as money.

For its part, the federal government established the Freedmen's Bureau, a temporary agency created under Reconstruction between 1865 and 1877, to provide food, clothing, and medical care to refugees in the South, especially freed slaves.

Special boards were established to set up schools for African Americans in the South, and black and white teachers from the North and South worked to help young and old become literate.

Some African Americans in the South were encouraged to move to Northern cities where jobs would be available. Extending the vote to blacks was met with hostility to Southern whites but eventually carried out and protected under Reconstruction.

The situation was made all the more difficult because of attitudes such as those of freedman Houston Hartsfield Holloway, who said "... we colored people did not know how to be free and the white people did not know how to have a free colored person about them."

In fact, many African Americans were quite prepared for freedom, as they demonstrated in 1865, and afterward by demanding their civil rights, the vote, the reunion of their families, education and economic opportunities.

In fact, for a time, scores of blacks were able to run for public office and win seats on all jurisdictional levels of government in the Deep South, though in the face of fierce opposition by racist whites. After the Civil War, the Union League was created and spread throughout the South mainly but not exclusively among the freed people.

Paid organizers, including freedmen advocates and anti-Confederates from Unionist clubs, went south to promote the League and loyalty to the federal government in the ex-Confederate states.

Many newly freed slaves, or freedmen, saw this as an opportunity to seek fair treatment and equal rights from the federal government and the state governments.

By the summer of 1867, thousands of freed people had joined the League and it became a strong political force. Due to fear of terrorist groups such as the Ku Klux Klan, the League met secretly in members' homes and at churches where they discussed issues of concern to them, including homesteading land, public school rights for their children, and securing opportunity to testify in court.

They were engaged politically by petitioning, striking and organizing campaign rallies. Increasingly because of the Union League, more African American political leaders emerged in both the North and South.

The Union League also exercised social influence and addressed agricultural concerns. It campaigned to end plantation agriculture and promote land ownership among the ex-slaves.

The success of the League angered terrorist groups like the Ku Klux Klan, which increased its violence against the organization. The League was a major target of the Klan during the 1868 presidential election, which was the first national contest in which African American men voted.

General Nathan Bedford Forrest, a high-profile Confederate military leader during the Civil War, was the first Grand Wizard of the Ku Klux Klan. But there's a part of Forrest's story that needs to be told.

Namely, he eventually saw the light, had a change of heart, renounced racism, closed down his Klan chapter, eventually worked to destroy the KKK and followed up substantially on his pledges to help advance the African-American cause to the Order of Pole Bearers, a social and black political group like the NAACP.

Soldiers come along, we all setting on the fence when a colored soldier ask her did she want to go with him and she said yes.

Interview with take no nonsense Aunt Harriet Smith, Hempstead, Texas, 1941. The WPA interviewed her at this time and here is what she had to say:

Harriet Smith: And you ask me any words you want to ask me about a slaves, you know, back, and uh, I can remember.

Interviewer 1: *Well Aunt Harriet about how old are you?*

Harriet Smith: Well I don't know Mr. I really don't know my age, only by the, the children telling me, of course. My ma died, and she, and she didn't know nothing about our age. But the children traced back from the ex-slave up to now.

Interviewer 1: *Well how old were you when you were* [Harriet Smith interrupts]

Harriet Smith: Well, I was about thirteen years old at the break up.

Interviewer 1: *Uh huh. Can you remember slavery days very well?*

Harriet Smith: Of course. I can remember all our white folks. And all the names of them, all the children. Call every one the children's names.

Interviewer 1: *Who, who did you belong to?*

Harriet Smith: J. B., the baby boy.

Interviewer 1: *Where was that? Where did he live?*

Harriet Smith: Back, out here in Hays County.

Interviewer 1: *Sure enough? How many, how many of, how many slaves did he have?*

Harriet Smith: Well, he had my grandma, and uh, and my ma. My ma was the cook, and grandma, you know, and them they worked in the field, and everything. I remember when she used to plow oxen. I plowed, I plowed oxen myself.

Interviewer 1: *Is that right?*

Harriet Smith: I can plow and lay off a corn row as good as any man.

Interviewer 1: *Is that right?*

Harriet Smith: Course I can.

Interviewer 1: *Well good for you.*

Harriet Smith: Chop, and chop, pick cotton. I used to pick, I've pick here since I been here. I've pick, pick my five hundred pounds of cotton.

Interviewer: *Knock out five hundred pounds.*

Harriet Smith: Knock out around five, five hundred pounds of cotton. Then walk across the field and, and hunt watermelons, pomegranates and [laughs]

Interviewer: *That's a* [recording unintelligible].

Harriet Smith: Yeah.

Interviewer: *Well Aunt Harriet, do you remember church times?*

Harriet Smith: Yes, I remember church time. I remember how [Interviewer interrupts]

Interviewer: *You remember during slavery times* [Harriet Smith interrupts]

Harriet Smith: Yes, I remember how our folks, they had prayer meeting from one house to another.

Interviewer: *Uh, the colored folks.*

Harriet Smith: Yes, I think it was,.. And over at the houses you know, they'd be in the section, a house, and at different places they'd go and we'd have prayer meeting. Ma and pa and them would go to prayer meeting. And dances too.

Interviewer: *And dances too?*

Harriet Smith: Yes. I've seen pa and ma dance a many a time.

Interviewer: *Is that right? During slavery times?*

Harriet Smith: Right. My grandma too. My grandma was name R. P.

Interviewer: *R. P.*

Harriet Smith: Yes. But she belong to the B.'s. [mumbles] That's, that, what she went by, her husband's name. Sure is, that's way back. Now in slavery time, there was my sister, my brother was a slave back then. And all of them stayed but me and one, one of the girls and she lives in San Antonio. A. T.

Interviewer: *A. T. She, she was your sister?*

Harriet Smith: Yes. She's in the young bunch. Sister Ida, and she was the next, brother George and sister Ida and myself were slaves. And the others was born free. And all of them, we the only two in slavery times.

Interviewer: *Well I declare. Did you go to meetings? Did you ever go to church?*

Harriet Smith: We would go to the big house, prayer meetings you know. We children would put us in the corner you know. We was dared to cut up too.

Interviewer: *Is that right?*

Harriet Smith: Yes, they'd carry us to prayer meetings.

Interviewer: *Well did you go to the white folks' church any?*

Harriet Smith: Yes. I went to Mountain City to the white folks' church many a time. You see the white folks would have church in the morning, then they'd let the colored people have church at their church in the evening.

Interviewer: *That was during slavery time.*

Harriet Smith: During slavery time, yes. During slavery time. I can remember that just as well as [Interviewer interrupts]

Interviewer: *Well what would the preacher preach about in them days?*

Harriet Smith: I don't know. He'd preach about you know, maybe something or another.

Interviewer: *They didn't preach like they do today?*

Harriet Smith: No. They wasn't educated, you know, and they uh, uh, would, would tell you how to do, and how to get along, you know, and how to treat the white people and so on. And they'd read the Bible then, you know, [mumbles]. Yeah, I remember all about in slavery time. Ma and them used to go to dances with the white folks.

Interviewer: *Well did they treat, did the white folks treat you good? Did you* [Harriet Smith interrupts]

Harriet Smith: Why, the B.'s?

Interviewer: Uh huh.

Harriet Smith: They was good to us. Good. They never whipped none of their colored people, our colored people. They'd take big saddle horse, Mrs. B's saddle horse, big gray animal, and she'd have them riding. Grandma would ride to Mountain City to church. They had white preachers there. Mr. P., he was one of the preachers that lived across from us.

Interviewer: *Well would the white preacher tell you to behave yourselves and be* [Harriet Smith interrupts]

Harriet Smith: Oh yes, they [Interviewer interrupts]

Interviewer: *Be good to your massa and mistress?*

Harriet Smith: Oh yes. That's what they preach. We sure, didn't know there was any such thing as God and, and, and God, you know. We thought that was a, a different man, but he was our massa .

Uh, our white folks, you know, preachers would refer to the white folks, massa , and so on that way. Preach that way. Didn't know no better. All of them, all of them would go up there to church. Then after we come to be free, you know, they begin to, preach us, you know. They, we begin to know, you know, there was a God and so on.

Interviewer: *Well, well, while you all were slaves did they teach you to read and write?*

Harriet Smith: Nuh huh.

Interviewer: *Did you all go to school any?*

Harriet Smith: Nuh huh. Uh, uh, they didn't know nothing about reading and writing. All that I knowed they teach you is mind your massa and your mistress.

Interviewer: *They sure didn't teach you any reading and writing?*

Harriet Smith: No, they didn't. No. When I picked cotton, I remember then picking cotton, farming [Interviewer interrupts]

Interviewer: *Well did you ever hear of any slaves being mistreated? That, were there any tales going around in those days about that?*

Harriet Smith: Uh, nuh huh, uh, yes, I know of times they, when they mistreated people, they did, and I hear our folks talk you know, about them whipping you know, till they had to grease their back to take the holes from the, the back.

Interviewer: *Good Lord have mercy.*

Harriet Smith: Them white folks were that a way. But them B.'s sure didn't allow their colored people be whipped. Their horses, their saddle horses, Mr. B's saddle horse and ma and pa and them wanted go anywhere, they, they rode their horses and the saddle.to Mountain City to church, and the children stayed home. Then, that on then, from one to another they begin to learn, from town preachers in amongst us to they'd prayer meeting.

You know from one house to the other you know how the house, like there's a house sitting here in a section, in line, you know, and people would come to prayer meeting. And then they, Sunday in the evening the white folks would let the preacher preach, let our folks go to their church for preaching.

Interviewer: *Well do you remember any of the songs they sang in those days at churches?*

Harriet Smith: No. I, I, if I had the books, I could maybe look, look and see. I know they sang the song, they sang the song, "Are We Born to Die?" They'd sing that in the colored church.

Interviewer: *"Born to Die." How did that go, you know?*

Harriet Smith: [mumbles]

Interviewer: *Yes, a little louder.*

Harriet Smith: Yeah, yeah.

Interviewer: *How'd it go?*

Harriet Smith: Yeah. They'd sing "Are We Born to Die?" [unintelligible] I was little. I would sit back. I never went much. We children, we stayed at home, parched corn and play you know. Little children.

Ma and pa and them and grandma would ride the horses, about two miles from our home, white folks' home, where they stay, and go to the white folks' church. I used to hear them laugh and tell it all the time, you know. We didn't know anything about freedom at all. There was three. There, there was me, and my oldest, next oldest sister and my brother George. He was, uh, they-they're all dead. All of them's dead but just two of us.

Interviewer: *Well, uh, can you remember when the war was going on?*

Harriet Smith: Course I can. I've sat on the fence at the time, me and cousin M., and cousin S., and all of us. Our yard had white picket fence around it. The road went right along by our house like this road goes along by my house. We sat on that, stood on that picket fence. All day long we seen them soldiers going back to San Antonio and different places. I had heard them they'd blow them bugles. Them horses was dancing and all just like that.

Interviewer: *Well what do you know.*

Harriet Smith: Colored soldiers`.

Interviewer: *Colored soldiers?*

Harriet Smith: Poor colored soldiers in droves. Went right along by our house. Our home, it was a two story house, the white folk's home, you know. And we stayed on the home until we bought a home, uh, it was over across the creek where we living.

Interviewer: *I remember a long time ago you told me about during the big break up, the soldiers came by and uh, riding horseback. And you all were sitting on the fence, you children. Can you remember that?*

Harriet Smith: Yeah.

Interviewer: *Lean this way* [Pointing to the recording machine] *just a little bit and tell about it.*

Harriet Smith: Yes, I remember, that's the, the, just, sit there, sat all day and look at them. They play the prettiest, prettiest music you ever heard in your life. And the soldiers would, you know. And them horses, they'd sing, you know. And them horses dart and follow the music just like that.

Interviewer: *Well I'll declare. Had them trained.*

Harriet Smith: Yeah, had them trained.

Interviewer: *Well what about this girl you told me about there one time.*

Harriet Smith: Well, N. P. was the one that uh, belonged to Mrs. P., the one that's our white folk's neighbors. And she got her arm ground off in molasses mill, feeding molasses mill.

Interviewer: *How was that? How do you mean feeding a molasses mill?*

Harriet Smith: Putting that cane in there for it to grind out to make molasses.

Interviewer: *Oh yeah. Ground out juice, uh huh.*

Harriet Smith: Yeah, juice. They had them wooden, what you call things, you know, mash the cane with them.

Interviewer: *And they hitch a mule to it wouldn't they?*

Harriet Smith: Yes.

Interviewer: *And he'd walk in a circle.*

Harriet Smith: Yes sir, yes. He'd walk in a circle.

Interviewer: *Kind of like a hay baler?*

Harriet Smith: It have a, it have, it have a lever to it, you know, and go around and around.

Interviewer: *Uh huh.*

Harriet Smith: We've made molasses that way. I've made molasses myself.

Interviewer: *You have. Well, now this girl got her arm ground off in*

molasses, uh, mill.

Harriet Smith: Yes, feeding the molasses mill, uh huh. That was the, that was the neighbor girl.

Interviewer: *Well how old was she?*

Harriet Smith: Oh, she was a great big girl. She was about, big enough to feed the mill. About ten or twelve years old I reckon. Maybe that old, maybe even a little older than that. The neighbors had a molasses mill, the P.'s. She made molasses for everybody nearly. That girl had that mill to feed. Cane, would have cane you know, great big piles, piled up.

She had to reach down and get that and put it in between them cork grinders and let it grind out and when that grind out, she'd pick up another handful and put in there.

Interviewer: *Well did they have good doctors for them in those days? Was, when it ground off her arm what did they do? How did they get her out?*

Harriet Smith: I don't, I don't know. I guess they carried her to, I, I remember Dr. M., and, and uh, Dr. C. I remember them.

Interviewer: *Well, when the soldiers came by what, where, where was she?*

Harriet Smith: Who M.?

Interviewer: *Uh huh.*

Harriet Smith: She was on the other side. She lived the other side of us. She was living, she was living with our white folk. But this road went right along by our white people's house. I can go right today where I was born there. And they was coming right along by the house and they'd all day for weeks at the time. Them soldiers was traveling going south to San Antonio. We children stand on the fence and looked at them. Oh they had the prettiest horses you most ever saw.

Interviewer: *Well now what, what did those girls, what would this girl M. do.*

Harriet Smith: M. P.?

Interviewer: *Uh huh.*

Harriet Smith: Well she, she fed the mill. She [Interviewer interrupts]

Interviewer: *Well I mean though when, when the soldiers came by.*

Harriet Smith: Why, she's on the fence there with us looking at them. She lived right across from us you know, and that was the road and she [Interviewer interrupts]

Interviewer: *Well I thought she went off with a soldier or something.*

Harriet Smith: She did. She went off with a soldier. Soldiers come along, we all setting on the fence, and uh, or standing at the fence, setting and a colored soldier come along and ask her did she want to go with him and she said yes. And she mounted one of them horses and [Interviewer interrupts]

Interviewer: *Right behind him huh?*

Harriet Smith: Uh, uh, no, rode a horse off herself.

Interviewer: *Is that right?*

Harriet Smith: That's right. We could ride horses. We could jump on them horses saddle sometime, ride them sometime. We learn how to do, I could stand flat-footed on the ground, jump on a horse sideways.

Interviewer: *Is that right?*

Harriet Smith: That's right, yeah

Interviewer: *Well you were a rider.*

Harriet Smith: Yes. All of us, all of we all was raised to ride horses. Pa had horses of his own, chickens of his own.

Interviewer: *Well now what happened to M. P. after she and this soldier* [Harriet Smith interrupts]

Harriet Smith: I, she went on with him. I never did see her and hear tell of her no more. She was going toward San Antonio.

Interviewer: *Going towards San Antonio.*

Harriet Smith: Yes. She rode on with them down there.

Interviewer: *Well, what did she do? She didn't even tell her mama she was going or anything, huh?*

Harriet Smith: She didn't have any mother.

Interviewer: *Oh, I see.*

Harriet Smith: Yeah.

Interviewer: *And it's all, she'd already been freed hadn't she?*

Harriet Smith: Yes, yes. That was the time the soldiers was going back you know after the freedom, back. And she'd always come over to our house and stay with us and play around. And she got on that horse and left that day.

Interviewer: *Well, can you remember the times right after the, after the big break up very well? Do you remember were times pretty hard then?*

Harriet Smith: Yes. Times was hard. We worked and our white folks wasn't mean to their colored people. They was different from, there was seven brothers of them. Old man S. B., and J. B., and B. B. And they had one more B., that was name Kentucky Joe and so on. Whole passel of them. Seven brothers of them, I know. Some of them lived at Cedar Creek. Ma knowed them all and grandma knowed [Interviewer interrupts]

Interviewer: *Well what did you all do after the big break up? Did you all leave the place?*

Harriet Smith: No. We stayed on the place, and rented on the half.

Interviewer: *Oh rented on the half* [Harriet Smith interrupts]

Harriet Smith: Yes. All, all our white folks was dead. And the overseer was old uh, B., Tom, Ira B.

Interviewer: *Ira B.*

Harriet Smith: At Mountain City. That was our uh, uh, over, overseer over the place there, you know.

Interviewer: *And y'all rented on the halves.*

Harriet Smith: Rented on the halves till we bought our home across the creek.

Interviewer: *Oh you bought your home. About how long after the big break up did you all buy your home?*

Harriet Smith: Oh, I didn't buy. We didn't buy. Pa bought the home from old R., across the creek. And he stayed down there. And I used to stay with Aunt Rose an Uncle George. They was old folks, had no children, you know. They used to get me to come stay with them. And when I married they give me a home on the place.

Interviewer: *Well were they white folks?*

Harriet Smith: No, colored folks.

Interviewer: *Oh, colored folks. Well, how old were you when you married?*

Harriet Smith: I don't know, about seventeen, eighteen years old. Well maybe not that old. I didn't know my age. But ma and them knew. They didn't tell us though. We just guessed at it.

Interviewer: *Who did you marry?*

Harriet Smith: J. S.

Interviewer: *J. S. Had he been a, had he, had he been a, a slave?*

Harriet Smith: Oh yes. He was a slave. After the break up they sent him, he come from Blanco and bought a home over across the creek where we bought homes, adjoining our home. His father and mother did, you know.

Interviewer: *Uh, well, he, he had been freed then, I guess, the, uh, same time you had.*

Harriet Smith: Oh yes, yes. They lived at Blanco. They bought them a home over in the colony. R. had sold the colored people all the homes here. I don't know.

Interviewer: *Who was R.?*

Harriet Smith: A white man name R. lived right down the hill from us. They sold

P. B. a home, and uh, pa had a home, Uncle Dave a home. All, all of them just all of them [Interviewer interrupts]

Interviewer: *Well I declare. Uh, that was right after the big break up was it, uh?*

Harriet Smith: Mmmm. About two, three years after the break up.

Interviewer: *Huh, and you just had a colony of, uh, colored folks?*

Harriet Smith: Yes, that colony, where we, where I come from, has got homes out there. At Buellah they call it now. It wasn't nothing but woods when we bought it.

Interviewer: *And they call it Buellah now?*

Harriet Smith: Yes.

Interviewer: *Oh I know where Buellah is.*

Harriet Smith: Yes, yes, yes

Interviewer: *Did you know Mr. T. in those days?*

Harriet Smith: I reckon I did know Mr. T.

Interviewer: *Huh. What was he* [Harriet Smith interrupts]
Harriet Smith: He was a deputy sheriff there for a while.

Interviewer: [addresses someone in the background] *Quit H.* and [then-addresses Harriet Smith]. *Did you raise many uh, did the white folks uh, poor white trash and the colored folks have many fights back in the, after the big break up? Have many run-ins?*

Harriet Smith: No. We never had nothing to ran into, but wagons and teams.

Interviewer: *Well I mean did they have many uh, you know, quarrels and uh, fusses.*

Harriet Smith: No. No, they just have these whites, these B.'s that they kill our white, our, our boys, my husband and his brother, was poor white people. They didn't like. And let me see how that did come up. I done forgot now, you know, all about that you know. I know my husband was on his way from the cedar break.

Interviewer: *Well did the white folks meddle? Did the poor white trash meddle much with the colored girls in those days?*

Harriet Smith: Not, not, not at our home. I don't know where they did it. At other places.

Interviewer: *Well I did, I didn't mean at your home. I mean around though. Did you hear of any, anything like that going on in those days?*

Harriet Smith: No. Yes. [mumbles] Well, the girls, we didn't run with them. They had different classes you know. Girls run, colored girls running with white boys,

and white boys would come over at night. But we didn't associate with them [Interviewer interrupts]

Interviewer: *Well did much of that go on in those days?*

Harriet Smith: Very little of it. It's going on more now than it did in my raising up days.

Interviewer: *Is that right?*

Harriet Smith: Yes sir. Yes sir.

Interviewer: *Well I, I think this might have gone on.*

Harriet Smith: Yes. They, they uh, we didn't go with them. Didn't associate with their kind no how. It's going on more now than it did in my raising. My, my sisters and me [**Interviewer interrupts**]

Interviewer: *Yeah, you know that little J. Jr. across the street from you looks, he's got almost blonde hair.*

Harriet Smith: Yes.

Interviewer: *His hair's white looking.*

Harriet Smith: Uh huh. His mama, yes, his, his mama, Miss F., is his grandma. Yes, Miss F.'s son P. M. is his, is his father, her oldest son.

Interviewer: *Well her name's B. though.*

Harriet Smith: I don't care what her name is. Her name's F. B., but she married a B. But B. wasn't these children's father.

Interviewer: *Oh I see.*

Harriet Smith: Uh huh. M. was these children's father.

Interviewer: *Well now who was your second husband Aunt Harriet?*

Harriet Smith: Who was my second husband? Let me see, who was my second husband?

Interviewer: *You married again after uh, uh, your what's his name, Smith.*

Harriet Smith: Old man, old man, uh, oh, I married B. S., was my second husband.

Interviewer: *B. S.*

Harriet Smith: Yeah. And uh [Interviewer interrupts]

Interviewer: *How long did you live with him?*

Harriet Smith: Oh, around about a year I reckon, two years. He, he had a good, he had Indian blood in him.

Interviewer: *He did.*

Harriet Smith: Uh huh. Indian blood. And then my next husband was old man.

Interviewer: *Well now what happened to B. S.? He die or did you divorce him?*

Harriet Smith: He, he wouldn't sign the divorce, but I got my divorce from him just the same.

Interviewer: *You did?*

Harriet Smith: Yeah, yeah, he, he lived a long time after, after me and him married.

Interviewer: *Well after, after you separated from him who did you marry?*

Harriet Smith: Old man P.

Interviewer: *What's his name?*

Harriet Smith: Old man P.

Interviewer: *Uh, how old was he?*

Harriet Smith: Oh, he was, he was eighty something. He was older than I was. He was about, I, I was his second wife that he married.

Interviewer: *Well I, didn't y'all have trouble? Didn't you and he have a little trouble?*

Harriet Smith: Who?

Interviewer: *You and old man P. Didn't he kind of cut up and carry on?*

Harriet Smith: Yes. He cut up and carried on and I quit him. Come on back home.

Interviewer: *Uh huh. Did daddy get you that divorce?*

Harriet Smith: Uh huh.

Interviewer: *I thought so. What was the matter with him?*

Harriet Smith: Old man P. was all right. He was all right, but his son, that's what we had trouble with, A. He come to command the place, you know, tried to put me off of the place. He couldn't do it. I stayed there as long as I wanted to, and when I got ready, I come on home.

Interviewer: *Then who did you marry?*

Harriet Smith: Uh, let me see, who was the last man I married, old man C. over here.

Interviewer: *Old man C.*

Harriet Smith: Uh huh.

Interviewer: *Well did you and he, did he try to whip you one time?*

Harriet Smith: Yes, yes. He couldn't whip me.

Interviewer: *Speak a little louder Aunt Harriet.*

Harriet Smith: No, he couldn't whip me. He tried, but he couldn't. I put him [Interviewer interrupts]

Interviewer: *What, what did you do to him?*

Harriet Smith: [laughs] Put him outdoor.

Interviewer: [laughs] *Well he was about a hundred years old wasn't he at that time?*

Harriet Smith: I don't know how old he was. He was in the Army.

Interviewer: *In the Civil War?*

Harriet Smith: Yes.

Interviewer: *He fought in the* [Harriet Smith interrupts]

Harriet Smith: Yes, he fought in the Civil War.

Interviewer: *And you married him in the 1930s didn't you? In the 1930s?*

Harriet Smith: Yes.

Interviewer: *Well you see that would make him, that would make him close to a hundred any how.*

Harriet Smith: Yes, but you see, you know there was another party between him, me and him that's the cause of our trouble.

Interviewer: *Is that right. Was he running, was he chasing girls old as he was* [Harriet Smith interrupts]

Harriet Smith: Yes.

Interviewer: He was?

Harriet Smith: Yes.

Interviewer: *He just could hobble around* [Harriet Smith interrupts]

Harriet Smith: Just could hobble around. They was chasing him for his money, you know.

Interviewer: *Oh I see.*

Harriet Smith: Because he got, us see, he got, uh, when he quit the Army, got old, you know, he got his, his money, from the Army.

Interviewer: *Well the girls uh, uh, must have made a fool out of him.*

Harriet Smith: Yes they did. Got his money, all his money. He got sixty or seventy dollars a month, every month.

Interviewer: *Hmmm.*

Harriet Smith: Yeah, [mumbles]

Interviewer: *Well do you still go to church Aunt Harriet?*

Harriet Smith: Yes. I go to church all the time nearly. Our church up, the Methodist Church up there [Interviewer 1 interrupts]

Interviewer: *Oh that must be [*Harriet Smith interrupts]

Harriet Smith: At Saint Anthony. Yes, I, I join that church. After I come here we built that church, we built that church [Interviewer 1 interrupts]

Interviewer: *Well who is your preacher up there?*

Harriet Smith: I haven't never met him, no. This, this we got a new preacher here, you know. I forget his name. [mumbles] Me and J. belongs to that church up there.

Interviewer: *Is he a good preacher?*

Harriet Smith: I've never ask J. what sort of preacher he is. This Sunday I was preparing to go to the church, some of the folks from another place come, and I didn't go.

Interviewer: *Well what do you think about Reverend R. as a preacher?*

Harriet Smith: Well Reverend R., he's uh, Reverend R. is Miss F.'s preacher.

Interviewer: *Uh huh. Over at the Free Will Baptist.*

Harriet Smith: Over at the Free Will Baptist.

Interviewer: *He's just a good friend of mine. I just wondered whether you liked him.* [Harriet Smith interrupts]

Harriet Smith: Yes. He's a good fellow. I like him fine. He's been to my house.

Interviewer: He has?

Harriet Smith: Yes.

Interviewer: *Well he thinks a lot of you too.*

Harriet Smith: Yes. He's been to my house. I like him fine. Yes. Been to my house several times.

Interviewer: *Aunt Harriet, what, how has times changed since you uh, came to Austin?*

Harriet Smith: Hmmm. I don't know. Times is changed. [mumbles] We've had churches, and different things like that.

Interviewer: *Did you ever think you'd live to see the automobile?*

Harriet Smith: No. I never did think I'd ever live to see the automobile. And the thing is, that I heard talk of them. I heard my husband talk of them. He went North with a herd of beefs with some white folks and he seen them up there.

Interviewer: *Is that right? He was a cowboy. Well which husband was that?*

Harriet Smith: *That was J. S., my first husband, all of these children's father.*

Interviewer: *Oh, he saw, he saw automobiles then when he went up with the, a herd of cattle* [Harriet Smith interrupts]

Harriet Smith: Yes, yes. He'd come back and say, uh, I saw these airplanes and things.

Interviewer: *Is that right. And came back and told you about that.*

Harriet Smith: Yes. We didn't know what nothing was.

Interviewer: *Well Lord, he was killed before the turn of the century, before 1900 wasn't he?*

Harriet Smith: No. He was kill in 1901.

Interviewer: *1901.*

Harriet Smith: But he had been up North with a herd of beefs, you know, for cattle [Interviewer interrupts]

Interviewer: *Who'd he work for?*

Harriet Smith: Well he worked for different people. Worked, we worked for ourselves then. We bought a home of our own Yes from white folks [Interviewer interrupts]

Interviewer: Did you ever plowed in the field haven't you?

Harriet Smith: Sure, I reckon I did. Plowed and chopped cotton up there. I could drop corn just as fast as I walk that a way. Grandma too.

Interviewer: *Plow oxen?*

Harriet Smith: Uh huh, yes.

Interviewer: *What was the name of your oxen? Do you remember?*

Harriet Smith: Oh, I forgot them. One of them name Jerry and the other name Broad.

Interviewer: *Uh, named what?*

Harriet Smith: Broad, they called him.

Interviewer: *Jerry and Broad.*

Harriet Smith: Uh huh. Yes, we'd pop them whips and them oxen would go 'round there and plow. Yes, I, I don't know if my children ever seen any oxen.

A SOLDIER
IS MY BEAU.

The music of this highly popular song can be had at
JOHN J. DALY's music store, 419 Grand Str. New-York.

Sung with immense applause by : Miss Fannie Denham.
Miss Carrie C. Austin, Miss Hannah L. S. Reed.
Miss Harriet L. Smith. Miss Adelaide Anna Mahon. &c.

Oh ! a soldier is my beau, I would have you to know,
　And he's gone at his Country's call,
To fight 'gainst the daring. the traitorous foe,
　And he'll conquer or nobly fall ;
For, his heart's always right, he's as true as the light ;
　On his breast will be found his scars,
With his face to the foe, he will bravely fight
　In defence of the Stripes and Stars.
　　　　　CHORUS.

Solo　— Hip hurrah !　⎫
Chorus　— Hip hurrah !　⎬ Repeat.
　　　　　　Hip hurrah for the Stripes and Stars !
　　　　　　　Hip hurrah !
　　　God bless those brave men again and again,
　　Who fought for the Stripes and Stars !

There's no maiden fair but would, no true woman but should
　Give a place in her inmost heart,
To the hero who passing thro' fire, field and flood,
　Bears a patriot's glorious part ;
But no bright sunny smile should the moments beguile,
　Or shine through the dungeon bars,
That imprison the heart of the caitiff so vile,
　Who loves not the Stripes and Stars.　　Chorus.

Oh ! may Heav'n protect my beau from the wiles of the foe,
　And spare him his bride to claim !
Let victory crown him where e'er he may go,
　'Till he win an immortal name ;
And with true courage nerved for the cause he has served,
　Let him haul down the Stars and Bars ;
For, this Union it must and it shall be preserved,
　And supreme wave the Stripes and Stars !
Let victory crown him where e'er he may go,
　'Till he win an immortal name ;
And with true courage nerved for the cause he has served,
　Let him haul down the Stars and Bars ;
For, this Union it must and it shall be preserved,
　And supreme wave the Stripes and Stars !

Solo　— Three times three :　⎫
Chorus　— Three times three :　⎬ Repeat.
　　　　　Three times three for the Stripes and Stars :
　　　　　　　Hip hurrah !
　　This Union it must and it shall be preserved,
　　Hurrah for the Stripes and Stars !

H. DE MARSAN, Publisher. of
Songs, ballads, toy books, &c.
No. 54 Chatham Street, N. Y.

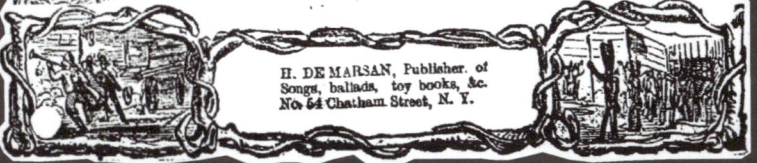

For more of this interview go to: https://www.loc.gov

Everything ⌄ | Aunt Harriet Smith | 🔍

African-American women played essential roles in ensuring the survival of blacks during slavery and of free black communities in freedom.

In slavery and freedom, black women established women-centered networks to serve the needs of the community. During the Civil War, women were usually restricted to traditional roles like cooking and nursing.

As an enslaved woman and later a free woman, Harriet Tubman performed this type of work, but, as a spy she worked side-by-side with men as Harriet Tubman, the secret agent, when she freed hundreds of slaves as a conductor of the Underground Railroad.

In one of her most dramatic and dangerous roles, Tubman helped Union Colonel James Montgomery plan a raid to free 700 enslaved people from rice plantations along the Combahee (pronounced "KUM-bee") River in South Carolina.

Early on the morning of June 2, 1863, three gunboats carrying at least 150 black male soldiers along with Tubman set out on their mission.

Tubman had gathered key information from her scouts around the Confederate positions. She knew where they were hiding along the shore. She also found out where they had placed torpedoes, or barrels filled with gunpowder, in the water.

Modern-era scholarship has sought to reconfigure the wartime and post-war history of African Americans as one of victimhood and suffering rather than optimism and agency.

To be sure, the destruction of slavery was a slow and uneven process, which generally followed the path of the Union Army's haphazard progress in conquering the South.

While some bond women leaped at the sight of the first colored Union soldier, others exercised extreme caution and stayed on the plantation for months or years after freedom became a fact. While certain bond women found new opportunities for work, education, and family life soon after ridding themselves of their masters, others suffered, became sick and died trying to build new lives.

As a result, African American men and women suffered greatly and died in unprecedented numbers between 1861 and 1865.

Black women used the chaos of the American Revolution, the War of 1812 and the Civil War to forge alternative and expanded paths to self-liberation.

They figured prominently in this "long emancipation" as they developed resistance strategies to challenge enslavement.

Beyond plantations, women escaped to cities and towns in both the North and South. They fled poverty, wealth, benevolence and malevolence alike.

Black women initiated their own liberation amid desperate circumstances. Mothers who fled during the Civil War took extreme risks, departing with young children in the middle of the night and walking for days until reaching Union lines.

And, finally, there was Mary Touveste, a free black woman working for a Confederate engineer in Norfolk, Va., who overheard plans for transforming the USS Merrimack warship into the C.S.S. Virginia ship.

After obtaining a copy of the plans, Touveste daringly crossed enemy lines to take this information to the Secretary of the Navy, Gideon Welles, which caused the Union to crank up construction of its own ironclad warship, the legendary U.S.S. Monitor.

Ain't got, didn't have but one and it died.

Interview with repeat that "Isom Moseley Boone" owned by two mistresses, Gee's Bend, Alabama, 1941. The WPA interviewed him and here's what he had to say:

Isom Moseley: My name is Isom Moseley. Raised up in old time without a mother. My old massa and mistress raised me. My massa was named L. M. My mistress was name B. M. Well, are you ready for me to talk?

Interviewer 1: *Yeah, that's fine.*

Isom Moseley: And, uh, and uh, after, my mother was a house woman, and uh, after she died, my father was a field hand, and white folks kept me around the house to tote cool water. Houseboy like.

And uh, they had two weavers weaving, had two looms running every day. Well you know I'd go out in the quarter to play with them childr, other children. And if I hurt one and they caught me, they would wear me out. Well the, the white folk told me, when they get at me, make it to the yard. Well sometime I'd go out there and get to playing, one would hit me, I'd get a brick bring it to him and to the yard I made it.

Don't nobody say nothing after that. And, uh, I, went on that-a-way and, uh, I

50

never can, uh, my massa was name L., you got that, and my, my mistress had a massa name, a young massa named L. M. He was a doctor. B. M., he was a farmer. F. M., he was a farmer. J. M., he was a farmer. Well, I had two mistress, B. M. and M. J. M. They was my mistress. And then, as I went on to tell you about, they made molasses way back then, and uh, they had no iron mills like they got now. They made wood, the carpenters made wooden mills. And they'd grind that molasses and they had a vat, big kettle to make it in, you know, And when that molasses was made, they had to pour that molasses in. No barrels at all. I never seen a barrel long then, nothing but troughs. And when you get your molasses made, they had plank to cover them troughs.

Interviewer: *Uh, you told me something about the way they made soap in the old days.*

Isom Moseley: Yes sir, I've explain that. Now I was large enough to tote water to the soap maker, put on ash hopper. They had a barrel, uh?.

You ready?

Interviewer: *You were telling about the soap making.*

Isom Moseley: Huh?

Interviewer: *You were talking about the soap.*

Isom Moseley: Now, now when I was a boy they used to make soap. Well I was large enough to tote water to the soap makers to put on ash hopper. Now they didn't have no barrels, they had boards, you know. And uh, them boards come in that-a-way, you know, that-a-way, boards was there. Well, all these here and you'd lay some crossway to hold the ashes. And then I'd tote water and put on that ash, ash hopper for the soap maker. Now he'd make soap for the whole plantation, and uh, make about two or three barrels. And along then captain, I ain't seen none, no bar soap.

They might have had some but I never seen none. And uh, they uh, had, uh, something dug in the ground, hole, deep hole and board up on each side, it was plank. Well it was about three foot deep I reckon, as nigh as I can come at it, and about eight or ten foot long.

Well, and about tanin leather. They'd lay a, lay a bark down in that hole, and then they'd lay, lay a hide over that bark. And then they would lay another layer of bark and another layer of hide, till they got it like they want. And then they'd fill that thing up with water. But now, now before they'd tan that, that leather, they had a place to put it in to get, lay a while and get the hair off it. And when they got done with that leather it's just like any tan leather, and they had a man there to make shoes for all us.

Now we was children, good size children, going about, that shoemaker make shoes for we children. And the old folks too. We had mighty good white folks, my memory, far as I can remember, you know, mighty good, mighty good. You know they must have been good. After the country surrendered, didn't none move, more move there after surrender. More moved on the place.

Interviewer 1: *What happened after the surrender?*

Isom Moseley: Sir?

Interviewer 1: *What happened after the surrender?*

Isom Moseley: What happened?

Interviewer 1: *Yeah.*

Isom Moseley: Well now, they tell me it was a, a year before the folks knowed that, uh, they was free.

And when they found out they was free, they worked on shares, they tell me. Worked on shares, didn't rent no land, they worked on shares. Now you know I was a boy, I'm about explaining to the best of my understanding.

They say they worked on shares. I think they said it was, was it fourth, or third I think. They got a third, I think they say, what they made after surrender.

Interviewer 1: *How many children do you have?*

Isom Moseley: Me?

Interviewer 1: Yeah.

Isom Moseley: Ain't got, didn't have but one and it died. None but one and it died. Now we was living twenty mile this side of Selma, in Dallas. That where I was birthed, I weren't birthed down here. No sir, I weren't birthed down here.

Interviewer 1: *How old were you when you came into Gee's Bend?*

Isom Moseley: How old I was? Seventeen year old. Seventeen year old and I come in the Bend here. A man here name, J. P. was here when I come, but the first owners of this place, that I don't know nothing about it but I heard the older peoples, M. P. Now uh, uh, C. Gee was the first owner. But that was what old man M.'s brother-in-law, tell me. Well, after old man Gee, M. took place, M. P. And then that's when I come here. They say his son, J. P., I don't know nothing about old man M. and C. Gee, but old man J. P., he was, he was a good man. He stayed here, I stayed here with him. Then he died, he been dead for forty some odd year. And uh, another thing about him. No, he had ten wage hands and uh, four plowers and, and six hoe hands. Never had a ride over them the whole time. Now he'd get up soon of a morning and ride around. Now uh, what we would be, the sun be a half hour high before you left home, he'd be in the field. That he would. And you know he'd make good crops.

Now he'd go soon in the morning, about eight o'clock he done been all around to his renters and to his wage hands and making it out to the house. And late in the evening, he'd go back again. Now he had a colored man for his foreman and the old

hands and a colored man head of the plowers. That's what. Now he make plenty corn with them ten hands, and forty and fifty bales of cotton. And he never had no rider over them.

Interviewer 1: *What's the government doing for you now?*

Isom Moseley: For me?

Interviewer 1: *Yeah.*

Isom Moseley: They give me clothes, something to eat, and giving me five dollars a month. They treating me all right. I don't find a bit of fault on it. Yeah, I got, I don't have to buy no clothes at all.

Well I buy, they give me five dollars a month, I buy my uh, uh, flour. Well they give me some flour some time, and some sugar and coff, coffee, I'm a coffee drinker, and tobacco. I have that to buy, but clothes, things I don't buy that.

Interviewer 1: *You're about eighty-five years, eighty-five now aren't you?*

Isom Moseley: Sir?

Interviewer 1: *You're about eighty-five years old?*

Isom Moseley: Yes sir, eighty-five. And they treating me fine, I don't find a bit of fault on it. I ain't had no clothes to buy since I been on the project. And I've been on it I think, about nine, about eight or nine years I believe. [Recording tape gets stuck]

Female slaves were aware that their masters needed and relied on their childbearing abilities to boost the slave population.

Bearing this in mind, enslaved women resisted performing this duty. They resorted to all forms of tactics from avoiding having sex to ending their pregnancies. Young mothers knew they would eventually be separated from their children.

If they had daughters, the mothers realized that sexual assault would be their lot in life just as it had been in theirs.

They worked to avoid this horrible fate for their daughters by actively seeking to protect their children from the nightmare of slavery. Often, they did what they felt compelled to. The mothers would take action by killing their newborn infants to keep them from being raised into slavery.

Such was the textbook case of Margaret Garner, a mother who killed her own daughter when she was discovered seeking to escape slavery with her children.

Garner's story inspired Toni Morrison's 1988 novel Beloved and a film of the same name as well as several theatrical plays and productions.

For more of this interview go to: https://www.loc.gov

LIBRARY OF CONGRESS

| Everything ∨ | Isom Moseley | 🔍 |

What you said Mr. President?

Interview with alway's ready "Lady Celia Black and her daughter, Tyler, Texas, October 11, 1974. Mrs. Black first arrived in this world on September 10, 1859. Here's the WPA interview and what's she had to say:

Interviewer: *Just like to ask you a few questions about your early life.*

Celia Black: Yes sir.

Interviewer: *Uh, uh, how, about from the time you were born and your schooling, and you go ahead and tell what you might and we might ask you a few more questions.*

Celia Black: Oh, I had my birthday. My birthday I had a, a nice time. I had a nice time. I enjoyed it. I enjoyed it, enjoyed all the good nice white people that was there, and the President was there and his, his wife, and shook hands with me, and just, I don't know. I just enjoyed it. I did. I enjoyed it. Was so many people

there. Oh, and I been thinking, if I had, uh, oh I had, had to many names to recognize to go on the air. I didn't think I'd be able to recognize enough to go on the air. Well, I've always have been, been a woman that would carry myself in a way that white and colored both of them would care for me. Well if my, my colored or whites had called for me to do anything, have anything to do with them, I's always there ready. Ready. Clean, care for myself, clean, and I always tried to treat them nice and I was good to them, I was good to the children, and I, I just couldn't be no better to them than I was. And I could, I didn't care when they call for me to do anything, I was right there ready to do it because I'm going to try to do what I could.

Everybody knows. So that's the way I carried myself. And that's, I'm so proud to know that I been recognized enough to, they care for me. Oh, and in Texas and, in the United States. I'm thrilled and proud to know that I'm cared for in the United States. Oh, oh, that I'm an old poor worn out colored woman down here and can't help myself. If I was up, why I could go cut hair. I'd always be ready. I be ready. I'd be ready to help. Oh God, it's true.

I'd help white or colored. I'd be ready to help. So, I'm down now and can't, but I've got a good desire. I've got a good mind. Oh, to be at home, I trying to do what I can, by the help of the Lord. If I can't do, if I can't do, I can speak well. I can speak well, oh, trying to help. Oh, as I can speak well of trying to help, oh, in my speech. And I trust my Heavenly Father. If I can be honored enough to keep my, oh, keep my recommendation, reputation up as long as the good Lord will help me, let me, spare me. As long as He spare me.

Interviewer: *Well you're, you're speaking of your, of your uh, birthday celebration. Do you remember anything about your folks talked about, back when you were born and, and that days?*

Celia Black: Do what?

Interviewer: *And, back, your mother telling about from the time you were born and where you were born at?*

Celia Black: Born?

Interviewer: *Yes.*

Celia Black: *I don't understand.*

Celia Black's Daughter: *Celia. Tell him about when you were a little baby and a little girl.*

Celia Black: Ma'am? Oh. When I was a baby I, well I, I couldn't remember nothing. I couldn't remember nothing from when I was a baby. No sir.

Interviewer: *You remember your mother talking about it though don't you?*

Celia Black: Yes sir.

Celia Black's Daughter: *Mama, You remember when you used to, tell him* *about the days when you was uh, baby girl and you used to ride the oxen and things.*

Celia Black: Yeah. Oh, my grandfather had some big old oxen. He had one with, uh, big with wide horns. Oh, looked like a house. [laughs] Wide horns, and, and, and I used to set up there in between them horns. And he, his name was Corley. His name was Corley. And the other one was named Let. Oh. And grandpa and them drive them to church, and he carried us where he went. And put us children in the, in the old, old ox wagon and carry us on his chest just as big as he was in a carriage. And, and I'd get up there and on, and on Corley, clinging on Corley's horns, and sit up there. Sit up there just as big as I was setting in a house.

Well, the furthest of my grandfather went go get lumber. Want to get some lumber, and he had to go across the river. It was in the summertime, in June, and the, old oxen got hot. They got hot. Oh, and then, uh, when we knowed anything, grandpa knowed anything, them old oxen done run off in, runned off in the river with us, with us, with that, with that wagon. And, and there I sat up there in the old, old Cor, old Corley's horns, horns. Sit up in old Corley's horns. Oh, and he's wading through the water, and I was setting up in there. I stayed in there too. I held to his horns. I held to his horns. I didn't fall off in the river. I held, I'm telling you, yes I did. Oh, oh, my grandpa was just a whipping with that whip, trying to get them out of that uh, river. And we was, and old Corley was coming through. They come out too. Yes they did.

Celia Black's Daughter: *Celia? Tell him about when you were born in Mrs. C.'s bed.*

Celia Black: I did. I was born next to a rich white woman. I sure was. She wasn't no poor woman. No, she wasn't. Her husband was living then. Oh, she wasn't no poor woman. Mama, she, she brought my mother up here from South, oh from one the other, in this country. She brought my mother here in Texas, when she was young.

Oh, my mother was young. She wasn't grown. Oh, she brought her here. Oh, way up to Texas to get grown. Oh, we've heard, we've heard tell. Oh. Well, my pa, my father and that, they, hired him to help her. Her white man, was name Mr. R. Mr. R. was a white man, and papa, papa was a a boy. And he raised, Mr. C.'s boss, uh got, hired him to be his yard boy.

When mama, she went at Mrs. C.'s here, uh a house of girls there. Papa and mama got, got together somehow. I don't know how they got together. But anyhow, my, my papa and then mama, uh. Mr. C. hired, my father be a yard boy. He stayed there till he was a grown young man too, with Mr. C. There they kept up her yard and kept her house, her yard and her horses.

Interviewer: Oh.

Celia Black's Daughter: *And you was born in Mrs. C.'s bed?*

Celia Black: *Huh?*

Celia Black's Daughter: *Were you born at Mrs. C.'s?*

Celia Black: I was born right be, behind Mrs. C.'s on a Tuesday morning, my mother said. My mother said it was on a Tuesday morning. Mama. I was born right behind Mrs. C.'s, in her bed. She always, my mother always slept with Mrs. C. when she was young, was young, before she was married. And Mrs. C., after she was married, my papa, Mrs. C. wouldn't, wouldn't agree for my papa to take her away from there. No, she wouldn't. She wouldn't agree for her to try and take her away from there.

Oh, oh. In them days, them days the white people had control over the, when they had, uh, uh, uh colored help, they wouldn't hardly, wouldn't agree, agree for you to take them away from them.

Then, and my, Mrs. C. brought my mother to this country, she wouldn't let no, wouldn't let, wouldn't let nobody take, take her away from there. She raised here there, with, with her children, with her children. She raised her there with her boys and girls. She didn't have but one girl. Oh, but she had five or six boys. She had, had, she had five boys, Mrs. C. did. Oh, but mama was just the only one, uh, only, and uh, Mrs. C.'s girl, she didn't have but one girl, and she, and she was a little. She was little. She wasn't no big girl. Oh. Oh, but she stayed there till, till she got to be a young missy. Oh, with, with, with mama, mama and then, uh, I was a, she growed up to a big girl when I was grown. Before she, ever think about time to get around amongst her boys.

Celia Black's Daughter: *Mama, you remember Abraham Lincoln?*

Celia Black: *Oh, ma'am?*

Celia Black's Daughter: *You remember Abraham Lincoln, the President?*

Celia Black: *Who?*

Celia Black's Daughter: *Abraham Lincoln.*

Celia Black: Oh, I heard my mother talk about him and my father, but I never did know him. I didn't ever know him myself, but I hear them talking about him all time.

Celia Black's Daughter: *What did they say about President Lincoln?*

Celia Black: Oh well, they, they give him a good name. They give him a good name. Oh, pretty good name. They give him a pretty good name. There's another one I know but I done forgot it, forgot his name. I just, Abraham Lin, Abraham Lincoln, that's it. Oh, oh, Abraham Lincoln. They thought Abraham was, was the best, they thought, everybody thought Abraham was the best President there was. They thought he was the very best. Oh.

Interviewer: *Did you, uh, do any, uh, picking geese for feather beds and things like that in them days?*

Celia Black: Did I have any? I wasn't nothing but a kid. I didn't, didn't, you know, didn't have sense enough to think like I gots now. I didn't have sense to think. Nothing but just to play in the block with the children. I didn't know nothing, know nothing about them, none, none of the Presidents.

Interviewer: *You didn't pick cotton or nothing?*

Celia Black: No, no sir I didn't. Oh until Mrs. C. raised me up, to be a young, missus. That's the only time I knowed anything about courting. And then, and then my papa had this, oh, to marry her. Mrs. C. didn't want him to have her then. Didn't want him to marry her then.

Celia Black's Daughter: *He said did you ever pick cotton.*

Celia Black: To marry.

Celia Black's Daughter: *Celia.*

Celia Black: Ma'am.

Celia Black's Daughter: *Did you ever pick cotton out in the fields?*

Celia Black: *Uh huh.*

Celia Black: Oh, good gracious alive. Pick cotton. I was raised in the field when Mrs. C. left, got, got, my ma and my, I was raised in the field after I growed up and got away from Mrs. C. Oh, I didn't do nothing but work in the field. Worked in the field, goodness, goodness, every year I would go out and work for myself. We'd go, my, me, and my husband would go out, out West and pick cotton. Pick cotton. Go out West every year. We wouldn't miss a year going out there picking cotton.

Interviewer: *Well that was hard work. Didn't you have some entertainment, do any dancing or anything?*

Celia Black: Huh?

Celia Black's Daughter: *You dance, didn't you mama?*

Interviewer: *When you were young?*

Celia Black: Ma'am?

Celia Black's Daughter: *Did you dance?*

Celia Black: Dance?

Celia Black's Daughter: *Yeah.*

Celia Black: Oh. I used to dance, but I don't do it now. No, I don't dance now. I try my best to serve my massa . I'm trying my best to serve my Heav, Heav, Heavenly Father. Try, trying my best to serve God. Oh, I ain't, I don't study about no man, no dancing now.

Celia Black's Daughter: *He wants to know mama, if you danced in your young days?*

Celia Black: Oh, in my young days? Yes. Oh, I went to balls when I was young. Oh, when I was young I went to dances. I didn't tell, I ain't gonna tell no lies. I went to dances when I was young. Oh.

Celia Black's Daughter: *Celia.*

Celia Black: Ma'am?

Celia Black's Daughter: *Do you remember going to town when you were young? Were there any big buildings back then?*

Celia Black: Who?

Celia Black's Daughter: *Big building, mama. When you went to town when you were young, were the streets dirt? When, did you go to town in a wagon when you were a young girl?*

Celia Black: I don't know.

Celia Black's Daughter: *Mama, you know you used to tell us you used to go to town in the wagon.*

Celia Black: Oh, oh. Oh, we used to go in, in a horse wagon. I thought you was talking about something else. Oh, yeah we used to go in the wagon.

Celia Black's Daughter: *Celia, did you ever see a stage coach?*

Celia Black: Ever see what?

Celia Black's Daughter: *A stage coach.*

Celia Black's Daughter: *A stage coach, where the people rode in the stage coach and the horses pulled them? Did you ever see one?*

Celia Black: Yes, I did. You call them in such a funny name, that I didn't know, know what you was talking about.

Celia Black's Daughter: *What did you call them?*

Celia Black: I call them horses. Horses. Mules and horses. Mules and horses. That's what they, what my, my grandpa call them. Hor, mules and horses.

Celia Black's Daughter: *What, what did Mr. and Mrs. C. ride in when they would go somewhere?*

Celia Black: What, in a, in carriage, what they called it. Carriage.

Celia Black's Daughter: *Carriage. You know, you've seen those carriage, you know.*

Interviewer: *Yes, I know.*

Celia Black: She ride in what she called a carriage. It's what the, what the, what Miss C. and them, A big old thing look like a, a, look like a cart, look like a cart.

Interviewer: *Did you hear anything about the uh, uh Indians in the days when you were young and the things that they did? The Indians?*

Celia Black: No, no, Lord no.

Celia Black's Daughter: *He's talking about Indian, mama, the Indian people. The people.*

Celia Black: Oh. I have seen them, but I didn't know them. I've seen them, but I didn't know nothing about them. Never did. I never did get any kind of, any kind of, no contact with them, with them. I never did.

Interviewer: *The Indians were pretty well gone at that time down here I think. But not farther north. Is there anything else that you want me to put there?*

Celia Black's Daughter: *Whatever you'd like. A few many more birthdays.*

Celia Black: Well.

Interviewer: *And we'll come up in the Panhandle. So we'll be thinking of you.*

Celia Black: Well.

Interviewer: *We'll be thinking of you.*

Celia Black: God bless you all.

Interviewer: *Good bye.*

Celia Black: Good bye. You, you folks are leaving here. If, if we don't meet in this, this world, then I hope we'll meet in yonder world. Meet in the new world.

Interviewer 1: *Well tape ends in the middle of a sentence.*
END OF RECORDING TAPE

For more of this interview go to: https://www.loc.gov

Everything ∨ | Celia Black | 🔍

In 1852, former slave and abolitionist Frederick Douglass posed a question to the audience who gathered to hear him celebrate the signing of the Declaration of Independence.

"What, to the American slave, is your Fourth of July? I answer: a day that reveals to him, more than all other days in the year, the gross injustice and cruelty to which he is the constant victim… This Fourth of July is yours, not mine. You may rejoice, I must mourn."

In many ways, Juneteenth fulfills the dream behind Douglass' question. The holiday celebrates the date enslaved blacks in the westernmost point of the Confederate states first heard the words, "The people of Texas are informed that, in accordance with a proclamation from the executive of the United States, all slaves are free. This involves an absolute equality of personal rights and rights of property between former masters and slaves."

President Lincoln's Emancipation Proclamation was issued over two and a half years prior to the holiday and the Confederacy's surrender had ended the Civil War in April.

However, it was not until June 19, 1865, that the order to end slavery arrived in Texas with sufficient military backing to enforce it. The spontaneous celebration, which followed this announcement, was the first Juneteenth.

Since then, June 19th has been celebrated annually as the end of slavery in the United States, although the federal government has yet to recognize Juneteenth as a federal holiday.

Juneteenth endured the suppressive efforts of the Jim Crow era and the hardships of the Great Depression to be seized and expanded during the Civil Rights Movement in the 1960s.

Its form varies from parades showcasing black African diaspora dance and music to community barbecues and from public lectures to private retellings of families' oral histories. Juneteenth may still be a new word to some Americans but it has been a day to remember black histories and celebrate black culture for over 150 years.

Historical accounts tend to frame the struggles of black and Native Americans as allied but separate: Native peoples were genocidally disappeared to be replaced by white landowners who then enslaved African Americans.

But indigenous peoples never vanished. They endured, survived and have been present and participants throughout all of American history, through hundreds of years of racist and genocidal policies.

For two and a half centuries, their stories have overlapped and intertwined with those of blacks. This includes tales of slavery and Juneteenth. Although often posthumously flattened into binary categories of black or Native, multiracial research and figures fill American history.

Crispus Attucks, the first person killed in the Boston Massacre, was of both African and Native (Nipmuc or Wampanoag) descent.

Pioneering 19th-century sculptor Edmonia Lewis was both Mississauga Ojibwe and Afro-Haitian.

In Galveston, Texas, the 250,000 enslaved people who were freed on Juneteenth were indigenous, black, and multiracial. Over the course of two centuries, an estimated two to four million indigenous Americans were subsumed into the same global system of slavery, which brought 10 million Africans to the Americas.

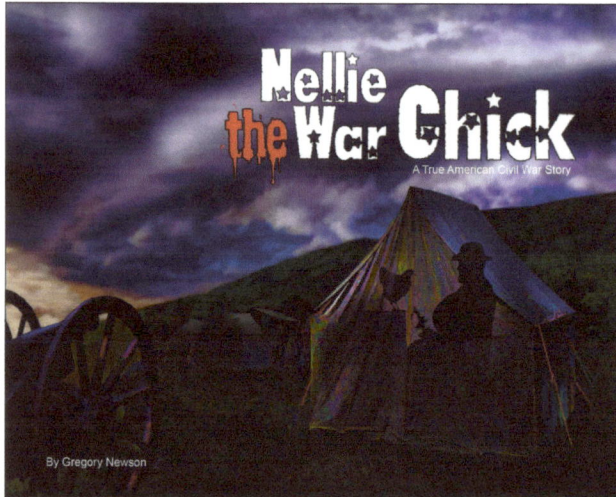

Nellie the War Chick
A True American Civil War Story
By Gregory Newson

This is a family book about Robert E Lee's pet chicken Nellie and his body servant, cook William Mack Lee.

This true civil war story is being told by the chicken, so its absent of politics and meanness. She quest for only for a life of purpose. As it's seems that General Lee favors the company of animals as he encouraged his soldiers to be beasts on the battle field.

Get Forrest
By Gregory G. Newson

GRAPHIC HISTORY

The truth about the wizard in the saddle Nathan Bedford Forrest and his black Confederates

There is a continuing story about the president of the confederacy Jefferson Davis and his wife Varina Howell that's not told in our history books. The expression about the black sheep in the family is real in this true story about an African American boy named Jim Limber who was adopted by the Jefferson Davis family.

Learn about the over 100 slaves that ran two plantations and about the spies Inside his household that contributed to the confederacy defeat.

But most of all take a close look at Varina, who does not look to be of European descent.

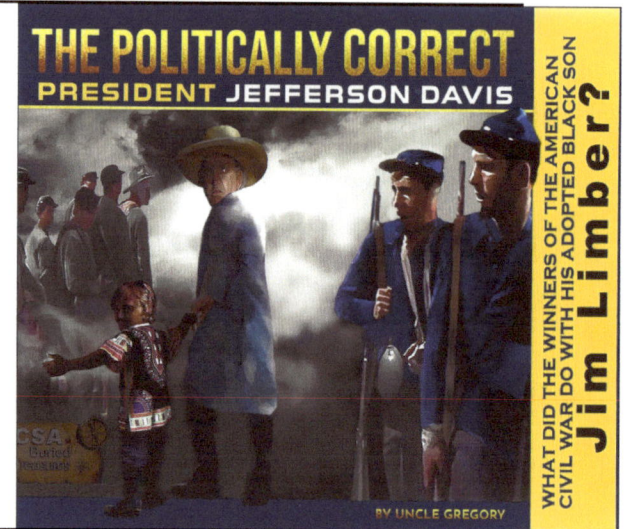

THE POLITICALLY CORRECT PRESIDENT JEFFERSON DAVIS

WHAT DID THE WINNERS OF THE AMERICAN CIVIL WAR DO WITH HIS ADOPTED BLACK SON **Jim Limber?**

BY UNCLE GREGORY

Why are we still fighting this war today it's because the truth has been suppressed by the winners of the war. This book is about Nathan Bedford orrest and his 45 volunteer slaves that went to war with him. And seven of them was his personal escort bodyguards.

But the remarkable thing is, as a leader he brought all back Black soldiers home alive at the end of the war. Learn the truth about the two klu Klux klan's.

Heroes by Force

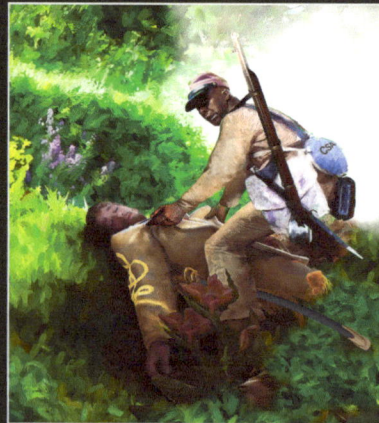

A list directory of African-Americans who served the Civil War Confederacy

Gregory G. Newson

The primary aim of this book is to celebrate the service of all African Americans who served in the Confederacy, whether they enlisted, were drafted or were ordered to serve by their masters.

Many are baffled as to why African Americans would fight for the Old South. The possibility of a brighter future: something well worth fighting for and risking one's life as a slave, whose motivations differed from those of free African Americans in this context.

Heroes do not ask for permission to be heroes. And many wanted respect and rather face a bullet than the lash.

www.ingramcontent.com/pod-product-compliance
Lightning Source LLC
Chambersburg PA
CBHW040805300326

41914CB00064B/1614